T0279450

Singin' in the Rain

OXFORD GUIDES TO FILM MUSICALS

Dominic Broomfield-McHugh, Series Editor

Love Me Tonight
Geoffrey Block

Singin' in the Rain
Andrew Buchman

La La Land
Hannah Lewis

Singin' in the Rain

ANDREW BUCHMAN

OXFORD
UNIVERSITY PRESS

OXFORD
UNIVERSITY PRESS

Oxford University Press is a department of the University of Oxford.
It furthers the University's objective of excellence in research, scholarship,
and education by publishing worldwide. Oxford is a registered trade mark of
Oxford University Press in the UK and in certain other countries.

Published in the United States of America by Oxford University Press
198 Madison Avenue, New York, NY 10016, United States of America.

© Oxford University Press 2024

Library of Congress Cataloging-in-Publication Data
Names: Buchman, Andrew (College teacher), author.
Title: Singin' in the rain / Andrew Buchman.
Description: New York : Oxford University Press, 2024. |
Series: Oxford guides to film musicals series |
Includes bibliographical references and index.
Identifiers: LCCN 2024022785 (print) | LCCN 2024022786 (ebook) |
ISBN 9780197760031 (hardback) | ISBN 9780197791967 (paperback) |
ISBN 9780197760062 | ISBN 9780197760055 (epub)
Subjects: LCSH: Singin' in the rain (Motion picture) | Musical
films—United States—History and criticism.
Classification: LCC PN1997.S5133 B83 2024 (print) | LCC PN1997.S5133 (ebook) |
DDC 791.43/72—dc23/eng/20240606
LC record available at https://lccn.loc.gov/2024022785
LC ebook record available at https://lccn.loc.gov/2024022786

DOI: 10.1093/9780197760062.001.0001

Paperback printed by Marquis Book Printing, Canada
Hardback printed by Bridgeport National Bindery, Inc., United States of America

Contents

Illustrations

Figures

Musical Examples

Tables

Series Editor's Foreword

"My disposition improved immeasurably when 'Singin' in the Rain' became available on home video," wrote the late playwright Wendy Wasserstein in an article written for the *New York Times* to mark the fiftieth anniversary of the film. "The VCR— and then the DVD player—made it possible to get a dose of the movie's positive energy whenever I become melancholy."[1]

Wasserstein's emotional response and attachment to *Singin' in the Rain* reflect how many people feel about the film, and this accomplished volume from Andrew Buchman uncovers many of the movie's impulses, origins, and implications. Drawing on archival documents, including screenplay drafts, correspondence, the Assistant Director's daily reports on filming, and scores, Buchman reveals important new details on this beloved film's production history.

Buchman sets the scene in chapter 1 by showing how MGM came to make a film about making a film. After bringing the studio structure to life, he reveals how legendary producer Arthur Freed went about selecting the story that he would go on to commission from screenwriters Betty Comden and Adolph Green. Buchman explores how Freed created a unique atmosphere by "adopt[ing] Broadway methods as well as Broadway names, allowing many artists a degree of creative agency that was rare in Hollywood." This led, for example, to Gene Kelly (familiar as the star of Rodgers and Hart's *Pal Joey* on Broadway) eventually becoming co-director as well as star of *Singin'*, so that his experience and vision could have influence behind the camera as well as in front of it.

Kelly's revisions of the screenplay, made in conjunction with co-director Stanley Donen and of course Comden and Green, are the special focus of Buchman's second chapter. His use of primary sources brings to life how the fabric of the film evolved during its production period: instead of executing a fully realized plan, the content of the movie changed a great deal as they went along. For example, Buchman writes: "Exactly how to end the film remained an unresolved issue even after production began."

Kelly and Donen toned down some of Comden and Green's satire but made the movie more romantic. This helped to create the perfect vehicle for some of the film's most expressive songs and dances, including the legendary "Broadway Ballet." Buchman shows that much of the film's brilliance was created through judicious editing: "Aside from the ballet, every number is temporally economical if not actually brief," he notes. "The film proceeds from one reasonably logical episode to another, generally quickly."

It's often startling to discover, though, that most of the songs in the film actually come from other, earlier films. Buchman's fourth chapter uncovers the process by which they were chosen, how they were orchestrated by MGM's team of brilliant arrangers (including the legendary Conrad Salinger), and how adjustments were made to the soundtrack late in the day.

Lastly, Buchman examines the long and complicated reception of this film, from its initial advertising campaign through to its many quotations in later work. At the close of his final chapter he remarks: "*Singin' in the Rain* continues to make people of all ages just feel good." Years from now, the same is likely to be said of Buchman's concise, lucid, and illuminating study of this Hollywood classic.

Dominic Broomfield-McHugh
Series Editor
Oxford Guides to Film Musicals

Preface

"Love it or hate it (and few hate it), overrate it or underrate it, *Singin'
in the Rain* makes a perfect musical yardstick."
                              Jeanine Basinger, from *The Movie Musical!* (2019)

Watching the original film musical *Singin' in the Rain* (1952) together is still
a great family pastime. Gene Kelly's beatific solo dance in the rain to the title
song has become iconic. But many remarkable film musicals exist, as the
founding of this series of guides demonstrates. Why has *Singin' in the Rain*
in particular risen to such eminence, rated "just about the best musical of all
time," or close to it, by critics and aficionados, past and present?[1]

In 2019 the film historian Jeanine Basinger dubbed *Singin' in the Rain* "the
musical for people who hate musicals" because of its hybridity.[2] In addition
to containing "all kinds of different [musical] numbers" it works equally well
as a "very funny comedy," a "charming romance," and a "history of the transition to sound."[3] But Basinger drew back from calling it "the best musical
ever made, although many would argue that it is."[4] Compared to many other
musicals, she concluded, "it's safe. And it's simple."[5]

Screenwriter Betty Comden and her writing partner Adolph Green
credited the co-directors for the film's quick pace, more twenty-first than
twentieth century. "There isn't a wasted second," said Comden. "The important points are made in every scene, and then it moves right along."[6]
Many critics also admire the work of the co-directors, Stanley Donen and
Gene Kelly, often giving Kelly (who choreographed and starred as well) the
most credit for making *Singin'* exceptional. As early as 1953 director Claude
Chabrol called Kelly an auteur comparable to Charlie Chaplin in the pages
of *Cahiers du Cinéma*.[7] In the more measured language of the film department at New York's Museum of Modern Art (as reported in the *New York
Times* in 1962), within ten years of its premiere *Singin' in the Rain* was "generally considered his [Kelly's] most representative work."[8]

In a 1966 interview Kelly pushed back against the rising reputation of
the film, saying "Oh, I know what they say about 'Singin' in the Rain' being
the best, but it was 'On the Town' that changed the complexion of musical

motion pictures."[9] Kelly was fighting a rising tide. Over the years *Singin'* has kept up its international rise to transcultural propinquity, sparking sophisticated interpretations offering new perspectives on American cinema, social history, economics, and politics, earning a place in the musical film museum as well as in the public's hearts.

Producer Arthur Freed, co-director Stanley Donen, and the gifted creators of the musical score deserve more credit than they generally receive. Freed empowered the creative team he assembled, ruling with a relatively light touch. Donen, working closely with veteran film editor Adrienne Fazan and sound supervisor Lela Simone, fine-tuned the final cut with keen observation and imagination. Inventive arrangements, especially those by Conrad Salinger, Lloyd "Skip" Martin, and Wally Heglin, reshaped, updated, and enlivened a trunk full of songs dating back as far as 1929.

This book is not meant to be read in isolation but rather as a companion to the film itself. For the film's fiftieth anniversary in 2002 the film scholar Rudy Behlmer supervised a celebratory 2-DVD release of the film including outtakes, musical numbers from earlier films featuring songs recycled in *Singin'*, and several relevant documentaries. Behlmer also oversaw a 2-CD release of the film's soundtrack, including all the extant audio outtakes from the film. These include Debbie Reynolds's audio recordings of the numbers "Would You" and "You Are My Lucky Star," which in the finished film were dubbed by ghost singer Betty Noyes (see table 3.4 in chapter 3). Copies of these will come in handy in the pages ahead, although one can also make do with online resources, especially any complete version of the film in which time points can be made visible; these are provided throughout the text as guideposts.

Chapter 1 focuses on the genesis of the screenplay. An overview of the Hollywood studio system makes clear how atypical Freed's productions were at the time. Freed could emphasize quality and draw on significant resources even as the industry contracted overall. A summary of the actual salaries the creators and cast members received reveals a profound gender gap (Comden was the lone exception). The figures illustrate that *Singin'* was still a business proposition for Freed and his fellow executives as well as an artwork.

Freed envisioned the film at first as a romantic drama rather than a comedy, commissioning an outline for a full-length adaptation of a somber play from the 1920s, *Excess Baggage.*[10] But then he apparently changed course and presented the project as a blank slate to Comden and Green, with one condition. Freed had played an important part in the transition to talking pictures himself as an Oscar-winning song lyricist, working most frequently with Ignacio ("Nacio," or "Herb") Brown. He specified that the film's score would be based on a set of selections from this back catalogue of songs, including the title song. In modern parlance, *Singin'* is a jukebox musical.

As detailed here, Comden and Green struggled with the assignment at first, exploring and drawing on a variety of possible models, influences, and ideas, before completing a draft screenplay in October 1950. This bitingly satirical early script anticipates the finished film in many respects. But few of the writers' ideas for musical numbers survived. In 1993 screenwriter Betty Comden countered a critic's characterization of their style as "fizzy," "light," and "fun," saying "I think there's a deep thread of real feeling in what we do."[11] The writers supplied a gifted ensemble cast with appealing and plausible characters, dialogue full of memorable one-liners, and a storyline satirizing movies, movie makers, and the movie industry.

Chapter 2 provides a guided tour of how co-directors Kelly and Donen converted a clever, talky draft screenplay with minimal camera and shot directions and speculative suggestions for music and dance numbers into tight montages, some as visually witty as Comden and Green's wickedest words. Revisions continued during production, over seven months of alternating rehearsals and shooting days from April to November 1951. Extensive archival records document the many changes made, including major alterations to musical numbers. Eventually the numbers filled 40 percent of the film's length. The characters became less complicated and more likable, and the vignettes depicting Hollywood's star-making machinery in action became less satirical and more nostalgic.

Chapter 3 delves more deeply into Kelly's cinematically conceived choreography, discussing the methods Kelly and Donen employed to integrate musical numbers into the narrative. Kelly had a penchant for illustrating a word or phrase from the lyrics of a song in choreographic terms, and Donen displayed a gift for integrating a number further by judiciously intermixing diegetic and nondiegetic musical accompaniments in imaginative but quick montages. The resulting smooth flow conveys a powerful impression of integration from start to finish despite Comden and Green's deliberately episodic narrative structure. Just weeks before the film's release Freed ordered a series of cuts. Donen and Fazan deftly excised nearly twenty minutes from the two-hour-long first cut, including two musical numbers. They are laid out and discussed here so readers can make up their own minds about whether these elisions helped or hindered the finished film.

Chapter 4 details Brown and Freed's careers as successful West Coast songwriters during the decade before they joined MGM. Previous appearances of the songs in *Singin'* in earlier sound films featured notable stars from Bing Crosby to Judy Garland. Learning more about the elaborate processes behind making a musical sound film at the time makes the quasi-documentary history lessons in the film itself more meaningful.

Musical analyses point out motivic relationships between various songs and accompaniments. The "doo-dee-doo-doo" riff Kelly hums to introduce his famous solo rain dance to the title song, we'll find, is woven ingeniously throughout Conrad Salinger's orchestral arrangement. Narrative analyses explore how underscoring and images work together in big numbers like "Make 'Em Laugh" and "Good Morning" but also during quick but subtly sculpted transitions from dialogue to music and dance, for example in the fast-paced lead-in to the elaborate "Beautiful Girl" montage.

Chapter 5 presents a reception history of writing and subsequent art about *Singin'*. Its present reputation as a classic is a far cry from the movie's status when it opened at New York City's Radio City Music Hall in the spring of 1952. *Singin'* was popular that year, but it was riding on the coattails of *An American in Paris*, which won six Oscars including "Best Picture."[12] The initial publicity campaign emphasized the film's suitability as a family entertainment for children under twelve. Yet, between 1960 and 2019 mentions of the phrase "Singin' in the Rain" in books published each year increased tenfold.[13] The story of how that ascent occurred offers lessons in how popular entertainments acquire traditional cultural prestige.

Sampled, remixed, referenced, or recreated, this venerable film is entering a new phase in its reception history. Makers of subsequent films, stage and television shows, commercials, and music videos have drawn upon the film for inspiration. Comden and Green themselves wrote a critically panned but commercially successful stage adaptation in the 1980s. *Singin'* onstage has enjoyed a series of major productions in London and Paris and in regional theaters. Creative references to *Singin'* by other artists including pop star Michael Jackson, the makers of the situation comedy *Glee*, the Korean band BTS, and the singer, choreographer, and TikTok celebrity Dréya Mac have explored bits from the musical as signifiers for violence, racial tensions, sexual preference, and states of mind.

Acknowledgments

Thanks to Dominic Broomfield-McHugh and Geoffrey Block—exemplary scholars, editors, teachers, and mentors. Thanks to the staff at the New York Public Library at Lincoln Center as well as the Bloomingdale and Morningside Heights branch libraries, the Library of Congress Music and Manuscript Divisions, the Library of the Academy of Motion Picture Arts and Sciences, Boston University's Archival Research Center, and the University of Southern California's Cinematic Library. Special thanks to USC's legendary Ned Comstock.

My home librarians at Evergreen have been unfailingly gracious and helpful, including Jane Fisher, Lorri Trimble, Jean Fenske, Jena Rosen, Ahniwa Ferrari, and Jason Mock. The Evergreen State College and the Evergreen State College Foundation generously supported periods of research and manuscript preparation. Thanks to my colleagues, students, and friends at Evergreen and elsewhere who have treated me with incredible patience, offering sources and suggestions that moved the work forward, especially Nathalie Yuen, Pauline Yu, Sean Williams, Rebecca Raitses, Sandie Nisbet, Markly Morrison, Paul McMillin, Rachel and Frank Lopez, Pat Krafcik, Conor Kiley, Soap Khan, Linda Kahan, Karen Johnson, Rose Jang, Chico Herbison, Nathan Groome, Alex Gootter, Joshua Goodman, Judith Gabriele, Stacey Davis, Jon Balsley, Arita Balaram, and Gwenyth Allison.

This book is dedicated to the memory of our parents, Tine and Irv, who passed on their love of books and the arts to all four of us kids: Amie, Mariette, Timothy, and me.

1

Creating "a Movie about the Movies"

"Singin' in the Rain isn't just a musical; it's a movie about the movies.
And that, I think, is why it often ends up among the so-called art-
movies on critics' lists."

Geoff Andrew in his foreword to Wollen, *Singin' in the Rain*

Freed's Ensemble Formula

The actor Betsy Blair called Hollywood "a company town . . . everything
revolved around the filmmaking." She also singled out MGM producer
Arthur Freed as one "of a few [Hollywood executives] who actively fought
for quality and artistry."[1] Her husband, Gene Kelly, described Freed as a
Hollywood version of Diaghilev, the impresario of the early-twentieth-
century Ballets Russes, and Freed's roster of creative workers as something
like a theatrical repertory company.[2] The screenwriters for *Singin'* praised
Freed as well. "The Freed Unit was something quite special in Hollywood,
with conditions that permitted us to function somewhat the way we would in
doing a show in New York. The writer was not treated as part of an assembly
line," wrote Betty Comden and Adolph Green.[3]

Within MGM, executives headed production divisions, shepherding a
number of film projects in various stages of development at the same time.
These were described at times as "units." In 1939 Arthur Freed had moved
from writing lyrics to producing films at MGM; soon he headed his own division. Freed's projects shared the larger production company's resources—
sets, costumes, props, equipment, crews, and shops. But Freed had an
additional, discretionary budget. As long as his productions generated
profits overall he could take chances on new faces, spend something extra if
necessary, and keep hiring proven talents over and over, fostering the growth
of a select stable of artists.

Each Freed Unit film was a collaborative product of this unique com-
munity "with its own politics and personalities and legends."[4] Freed wasn't

Singin' in the Rain. Andrew Buchman, Oxford University Press. © Oxford University Press 2024.
DOI: 10.1093/9780197760062.003.0001

the only producer who made musicals at MGM, but he specialized in the genre he helped to create in the late 1920s and decisively updated in the late 1930s in films like *The Wizard of Oz* (for which he received no screen credit) and *Babes in Arms*, both of which appeared in 1939. After the hegemony of sound films was established, Freed and other Hollywood moguls often sought to hire people from New York who had already worked successfully on Broadway musical stage shows. However, Freed went a step farther. He adopted Broadway methods as well as Broadway names, allowing many artists a degree of creative agency that was rare in Hollywood. Freed also made it possible for talented workers to switch roles, for example allowing Kelly to write and direct as well as act, dance, sing, and choreograph.

A multitalented sextet created *Singin' in the Rain*. The film's producers, Arthur Freed (1894–1973) and Roger Edens (1905–1970), were both accomplished songwriters, pianists, and singers. The screenwriters, Betty Comden (1917–2006) from Brooklyn and Adolph Green (1914–2002) from the Bronx, grew up watching silent and sound movies. They honed their gift for satirizing Hollywood fads and foibles in live cabaret performances and continued to perform even after achieving success as writers. The co-directors included the film's biggest star, Gene Kelly (1912–1996) from Pittsburgh. Like his boss Freed, dancer and co-director Stanley Donen (1924–2019) hailed originally from Charleston, South Carolina. Freed's family had headed west, resettling in Seattle in 1908 when Arthur was thirteen or fourteen.[5] Donen left for New York after finishing high school in 1940, landing a spot as a dancer on Broadway in *Pal Joey*, starring Kelly as a handsome heel.

While Kelly was the best-known performer by far, all six had performed professionally. Freed sang in vaudeville in the 1920s and Edens played piano in swing bands in the 1930s. Comden and Green were actors and singers as well as authors. The writers and directors had already collaborated on two earlier films for Freed and Edens released in 1949, *Take Me Out to the Ball Game* and *On the Town*. "The success of [*Singin' in the Rain*] and its continued life over the years had much to do with our four-way mental radar," wrote Comden and Green, "Gene and Stanley's brilliant execution, and their sure professionalism while maintaining an air of effortless, carefree spontaneity. Also, one of the two directors gave a great performance."[6]

Comden and Green's strong but rough first drafts of a screenplay play a central role in the story of the making of *Singin' in the Rain*. Next, the co-directors participated in extensive revisions leading to a second draft to which Freed gave the green light for production. Kelly and Donen created all the final versions of the musical and dance numbers, transforming many of Comden and Green's words and ideas. Edens and Freed also played decisive roles in shaping the film. But it would be misleading to concentrate exclusively on these creative artists without describing the corporate culture within which they worked and from which they drew much of their subject matter. What is often described as the film's self-reflexivity (a film about filmmaking) can also be interpreted as a deeply nostalgic, if comic, look back at "Olden Days in Hollywood," when what became a global industry was still in the throes of creation.[7] *Singin'* was, first and foremost, a product of the still mighty, but increasingly vulnerable, Hollywood studio system.

MGM Studios: Big, Rich, but in Decline

Between 1925 and 1945 MGM, located on 167 acres (about 68 hectares) in Culver City northwest of downtown Los Angeles, grew into the North American film industry's largest and richest factory, cranking out a new feature almost every week of the year at its height.[8] It was vividly described by Scott Eyman in his 2005 biography of Louis B. Mayer, the final "M" in MGM.[9] There were thirty soundstages on the property, seven warehouses for props, costumes, and equipment, thirty-seven acres of outdoor "backlot" sets, ersatz jungles and rivers, and a private zoo where Leo the lion lived.[10] In 1944 six thousand employees entered the grounds via three guarded entrances including a main gate girded with Corinthian columns, the model for the gate to the fictional Monumental Pictures studio in *Singin'*.[11] In that year thirty-three actors were designated as stars, seventy-two were considered featured players, and twenty-six directors were engaged under long-term contracts. Up to eighteen pictures were typically in production at the same time.[12] About 2,700 people ate in the commissary every day.[13] The studio's film laboratory printed 150 million feet of release prints yearly, distributing product to its own national chain of theaters nominally controlled by MGM's corporate parent located in New York City, Loew's.[14]

In 1948 the US Department of Justice won an antitrust case, *United States v. Paramount Pictures, Inc., et al.*, in the US Supreme Court.[15] It took ten years, but by 1957 the vertically integrated oligopoly large film companies had devised in the 1920s was broken up. The court's decision wasn't the industry's only big problem. In 1947 there were 40 million radios in the U.S. and only 44,000 television sets. But that year another 178,000 TV sets were manufactured; 149,000 were sold. In 1948 production increased sevenfold to 978,000 televisions. In 1946, when the movie industry was at its height, 90,000,000 people went to the movies every week.[16] By 1950 that number was down to 60,000,000 per week and still declining.[17]

Building on preexisting radio networks, by 1951 three commercial television broadcasters based in New York City—CBS, NBC, and ABC—had signed up affiliates all the way to the West Coast and were well on their way to establishing a new media oligopoly, displacing radio networks and Hollywood studios.[18] In 1952, just two weeks after *Singin' in the Rain* had premiered at Radio City Music Hall, also in New York, Herbert Kupferberg reported in the city's *Herald Tribune* on a shrunken but still mighty MGM domain: four thousand employees producing forty movies a year at a total cost of about $50 million (roughly $600 million in 2024 dollars).[19]

In 1988 Thomas Schatz explored why the Freed Unit retained the resources that enabled it to turn out so many great musical films during an era when the movie industry was in a prolonged crisis. Led by the same consortium of executives since 1924, MGM clung tightly to the studio system that had served it so well, managing to hold on to its money-making theater chain despite court challenges through 1957.[20] According to Schatz, MGM was the last Hollywood studio standing. It continued to maintain a large, unionized staff of professional technical workers and a huge array of production facilities from soundstages to gargantuan backlot sets like the paddlewheel steamboat constructed for Freed's 1951 remake of *Show Boat*. While in 1952 MGM remained "the largest movie studio in the world," the film business was in a prolonged, wrenching economic and creative crisis, akin to the technological and social crises of the late 1920s, including the rise of the talkies and the advent of the Great Depression. Certainly, many of the fine craftspeople behind the scenes on the picture knew that the studio's days might be numbered.

As Schatz put it, "MGM produced eight to ten musicals per annum," "year after year," because "given its resources, the studio could ill afford *not* to" (italics in original).[21] Although its costs were extraordinarily high by industry standards and its profits therefore usually modest, in Freed's case the money was well spent.[22] Although the numbers can't be considered definitive, salary estimates from internal documents in the Arthur Freed archives suggest that the studio also profited by exploiting its working actors—not just during the years they were starting out but in Kelly's case, even during his years of greatest stardom and earning power. Of course, one can argue that the risk the studio took on justified their profits, which balanced out many losses on other projects. A quick look at who got paid what while the film was being produced follows.

Gender Inequities on the Financial Side

Singin' in the Rain was Kelly's twentieth Hollywood film. He was an established box office draw and received $3,500 per week from MGM for a maximum of forty weeks per year.[23] Both Kelly and Donen were projected to work a total of thirty weeks on *Singin'* during 1951.[24] Kelly's total compensation for *Singin'* added up to $102,083 for twenty-nine weeks and one day.[25] At the same time Donen was receiving $1,000 per week.[26] Among all US workers in 1951 the median income was $2,200 per year.[27]

Given his stardom and his triple role as director, choreographer, and actor, Kelly's seemingly generous compensation arguably still didn't match up with his importance to the film's commercial and artistic success. He brought both star power and authorial vision to the table. According to Kelly, his initial contract with MGM described him accurately as a singer, actor, dancer, director, and choreographer but offered him no additional compensation for filling more than one of these roles on the same film.[28] Letters to Comden and Green from their agent (who received 10 percent of Comden and Green's salaries before taxes) document a specific instance of Kelly going above and beyond the letter of his contract. Kelly met daily with Comden and Green during a crucial three-week period in the spring of 1951, turning their first draft into a camera-ready second draft screenplay. Kelly wasn't paid a cent for this work. He was still on obligatory leave without pay after finishing *An American in Paris.*[29]

Donald O'Connor, borrowed from another studio, held out for a fair share of his studio's fee for "lending" him out—$50,000. He ended up receiving $5,000 per week for eighteen weeks of work totaling $90,000.[30] While he told Roger Ebert that he also received the $50,000 fee his studio was charging MGM for lending him out, there seems to be no separate record of this transaction in the Arthur Freed papers, which suggests that it may have been bundled into his weekly salary.[31] Millard Mitchell as R. F. did all right at $3,125 per week for eight weeks, a total of $25,000, during a busy year.[32] In addition to starring in *My Six Convicts* Mitchell appeared in a Western also released in 1952, *The Naked Spur*.[33] Sadly, he died in 1953, aged just fifty, of lung cancer.[34] Doug Fowley as the film director Roscoe Dexter earned $750 a week over five weeks and four days for $4,375.[35]

The compensation for the supporting players reveals a glaring gendered pay gap. A salary of $750 a week, the bottom of the range for men in the cast, was the very top of the salary range for the women.[36] Budding star Reynolds received $350 per week for eighteen weeks totaling $5,400.[37] Hagen, although nominated for an Oscar for her work in her ninth film, didn't do much better at $500 a week for seven and a half weeks totaling $3,750.[38] Rita Moreno earned $750 per week for three and one-third weeks totaling $2,500, but her part was cut down and MGM terminated her contract later the same year.[39] Madge Blake, unforgettable as Dora Bailey, earned $450 for three days at $150 per day.[40] Comden was the lone exception to this gender pay gap. She and Green each received $1,750 per week.

Despite their 1950 deal to assign film rights to their songs to MGM, it appears that Freed and Brown received additional flat fees of $25,000 and $35,000, respectively, for their participation as advisers (and songwriters for the new song "Make 'Em Laugh") on *Singin' in the Rain*.[41] Freed's salary and bonuses as a producer were in addition to this fee, vividly illustrating how much Kelly lost by not receiving separate compensation for each of his creative roles. Like Comden, Green, and Edens (who co-owned their one original song for the film, "Moses Supposes"), both Freed and Brown also received ASCAP royalties on any ancillary recordings of their songs that the film inspired.

An Overview of the Genesis of the Screenplay

Although Freed compensated the writers of the Broadway hit *On the Town* and its film adaptation relatively well, he also employed lesser staff writers to develop properties, including *Singin'*. As early as 1948 the *Los Angeles Times* had announced that Perry Como "will probably be starred in 'Singin' in the Rain,' when that picture is made by Arthur Freed."[42] In 1949 Freed asked Ben Feiner Jr. to write a treatment (a story outline) for the projected film, based on a drama with plenty of music from the 1920s, *Excess Baggage*. The play had previously been adapted into a mostly silent film at MGM with some early sound effects in 1928.[43] It seems clear that even at this early

Figure 1.1 Poster for the film *Excess Baggage* (1928).

date, Freed was envisioning a storyline set at the dawn of the sound era. See figure 1.1.[44]

Although the film is lost, the script for the stage play survives.[45] It's a somber tale of a happily married showbiz couple falling into discord when one spouse becomes more successful than the other.[46] Elsa and Eddie Kane meet in a rainstorm, form a vaudeville duo, and wed.[47] Elsa is recruited for screen work. Established film star Val d'Errico's wooing threatens the pair's marriage. Then Feiner introduced a new plot element not present in the 1927 stage play: the transition from silent to sound movies. In Feiner's rewrite of Jack McGowan's play (retitled *Singing in the Rain*), the wife not only succeeds as a silent film star but makes the perilous transition to sound. A benevolent studio head has her take singing lessons and casts her in "the studio's first big musical."[48]

Feiner remade the ending into a happier one than that in the silent film, in which Elsa rushed into the theater just in time to save Eddie from nearly killing himself attempting a high wire stunt. In Feiner's retelling Eddie's vaudeville singing and dancing skills make him a natural for the talkies, too. He joins Elsa onscreen for a joyful finale built around a reprise of (what else?) the song "Singin' in the Rain."

Feiner wasn't the only additional writer hired by Freed for *Singin'*. Yet another writer, Jerome Davis, was on the payroll from March 27 to April

15, 1950; his role is unknown.[49] Comden and Green may not have known about these additional writers. In fact, they claimed that it was they who had come up with the idea of setting the story in the late 1920s, to make Freed and Brown's songs "bloom [again] at their happiest" moment."[50] In 1972 they also went on the record with their initial reluctance to take on the project. They preferred to write the lyrics to a set of new songs themselves and opposed working with Freed's back catalogue of old song hits. They even said they went "on strike" for weeks before getting to work, although it appears that they were actually being paid during this work stoppage.[51]

After learning that they had no right to refuse the assignment, "we began working on *Singin' in the Rain* like rats trapped in a burning barn."[52] Despite that frantic description suggesting enforced haste, the pair actually spent six months on salary in 1950 producing a first draft of a screenplay, a complete story but one containing only initial, sometimes sketchy suggestions for musical numbers. In October 1950 Comden and Green left Hollywood to develop a new Broadway revue (*Two on the Aisle*, their first collaboration with composer Jule Styne).

As explored in chapter 2, they returned for just three weeks the following spring, implementing a series of changes reflecting developments over the winter. Kelly and Donen contributed ideas to the evolving screenplay at this time. The quartet of editor/writers reduced the amount of repartee, perhaps unintentionally toning down the first draft's more pointed satire in the process. The quartet of revisers also shaved down supporting roles and eliminated dialogue providing backstories for the major characters. Two more movie stars, both highly proficient dancers, were added to the cast: Donald O'Connor and Cyd Charisse. The weight of the film shifted decisively toward musical numbers devised or revised by the directors.

Music and dance ended up occupying two fifths of the film's length. As examined in chapter 3, the studio finally mandated the removal of two musical numbers and a number of segments from scenes elsewhere, shortening the two-hour-long first edit by almost twenty minutes. For an overview of the project's genesis from start to finish see table 1.1, Drafts of the Screenplay for *Singin' in the Rain*.

Comden and Green had already written skits about "Olden Days in Hollywood" for their night club quintet The Revuers.[53] In an interview with William Baer the pair cited some of these skits as nuclei for their screenplay

Table 1.1 Major Drafts of the Screenplay for *Singin' in the Rain*

Date	Description
1949-01-28	Treatment, adapted by Ben Feiner Jr. from *Excess Baggage* by John "Jack" MacGowan[1]
1950-08-10	**First Script** by Comden and Green; marked "Temporary Incomplete"; with revisions through September 14[2]
1951-04-11	**"OK" script** [okayed by Freed for production][3]
1951-07-26	Draft of new finale by Joseph Fields (not used)[4]
1952-03-17	**Continuity Script** prepared for film editing (exact date unknown), dated March 17, 1952[5]
no date	**Composite Script**—Assembled from the "OK" script, manuscript and typed revisions, and Continuity Script pages. Earliest dated pages marked April 11, 1951; latest marked June 25, 1951.[6]

Sources: [1] Ben Feiner Jr., "Original Singing in the Rain-Cp rough draft of story outline from Ben Feiner, Jr.," January 28, 1949, Turner/MGM Scripts, 2642-f.S-1233, AL.

[2] Betty Comden and Adolph Green, *Singin' in the Rain,* first draft script, MGM script, August 10–September 14, 1950, Turner/MGM Scripts, 2642-f.1234, AL. See also 2642-f.S-1235 ("Temporary Complete," with revisions to October 5), Turner/MGM Scripts, AL; and Comden and Green Papers, Box 9, Folder 6, NYPL ("Temporary Complete," with revisions to October 14).

[3] Betty Comden and Adolph Green, *Singin' in the Rain,* "OK" [second] draft script, April 11, 1951, with revisions through June 25, Betty Comden Papers, Box 12, Folder 11, NYPL. See also Comden and Green Papers, Box 9, Folder 7, NYPL (with revisions through July 20); and Green Papers, Box 12, Folder 3, NYPL (April 11, 1951, also with revisions through July 20).

[4] Joseph Fields, Draft of finale, Turner/MGM Scripts, Folder 1241, AL.

[5] No authors listed, *Singin' in the Rain,* continuity script, CTR 1390, NYPL (this copy includes all music cues); and Betty Comden Papers, Box 12, Folder 12, NYPL.

[6] Betty Comden and Adolph Green, *Singin' in the Rain,* composite script, Comden and Green Papers, Box 9, Folder 7, NYPL. Possibly compiled in 1970 or 1971 for the script as published in 1972.

for *Singin'*.[54] In one, Green, playing a character named Donald Ronald, would mouth words to a scene. Another member of the group would recite the text out of sync, as in the "no, no, no / yes, yes, yes" scene in *Singin'* (at 58:49 in the film). In another, Green mimicked the effect of a poorly placed microphone, singing an original song, "Honeybunch," in which every other word was inaudible, as in the scene in *Singin'* in which Lina Lamont keeps turning her head away from a hidden microphone (53:10).[55] Kelly also traced the inspiration for the character of Lina Lamont to Judy Holliday's performances with The Revuers, recalling that "Judy used to do this dumb blond. A lot of that crept into 'Born Yesterday.'"[56] Holliday's Oscar-winning portrayal of the character of Billie Dawn in that film will be discussed further later on in this chapter.

Comden and Green's First Draft Screenplay (1950)

As in the final film, the first screenplay opens with the stars' arrival at a silent movie premiere, followed by Don's double autobiography. The hardscrabble rise through touring vaudeville shows depicted onscreen contradicts Don's noble words. Next a sequence counterpoints the first showing of the film itself with audience members' reactions to it. Comden and Green credited Comden's husband for the advice to combine several nascent ideas into one complex sequence for the film's opening.[57] Comden and Green proposed punctuating Don's autobiography with a song and dance for Don and Cosmo, "Fit as a Fiddle." This is the only musical number Comden and Green proposed that remained in place (albeit with revisions) in the final film. It's also the only song with lyrics by Freed in the score with music by someone other than Brown, and the only old song that had never appeared in a film before. Composers Al Hoffman and Al Goodhart collaborated with Freed on the song, released in 1932 as sheet music, recorded on 78 rpm records by artists in the US and abroad, and featured on radio broadcasts at the time.

Although it is this author's idea, not that of the screenplay writers, one way of parsing out the story is to see it as organized around a series of four new films created within the film, beginning with the gala premiere of *The Royal Rascal* (or *Royal Rogue* in some early drafts). This silent film is the latest in a series starring Lina Lamont and Don Lockwood, assisted by his sidekick Cosmo Brown. Work begins immediately on another silent film in the same quasi-historical romantic vein, tentatively titled *The Dueling Cavalier*.

Threatened by the tremendous commercial success of early sound films from other unnamed studios like *The Jazz Singer* (1927) starring Al Jolson, the fictional Monumental Pictures studio closes to retool and the same film is quickly remade with a soundtrack. But Lina's tough New York accent doesn't match up with her glamorous, refined onscreen persona. The soundtrack is also full of unintentionally hilarious technical flaws.

At Cosmo's suggestion, talented singer Kathy Selden saves the day, stepping up to dub Lina's dialogue and songs. The film is remade again as a thoroughly modern sound musical retitled *The Dancing Cavalier*. At the new musical's premiere, Lina's lip-syncing is exposed. Neatly mirroring the opening scenes, the story then jumps ahead to yet another film premiere, for a film starring Don and Kathy titled *Broadway Rhythm*.[58]

Comden and Green simply specified some kind of musical finale, without even mentioning a particular song as a candidate. In fact, Comden and

Green's first screenplay draft ended with *two* hazily defined but "big" musical finales. The first formed a part of *Broadway Rhythm,* the final film of the four films contained within the storyline at this point. The other was a suggestion for a final ensemble song and dance, presumably set on the stage of the theater where *Broadway Rhythm* had just been shown. If this seems complicated, hopefully table 1.2, containing scene summaries along with Comden and Green's nascent ideas for musical numbers in the first "temporary, incomplete" draft screenplay, will make things clearer.

More changes were made before this "Temporary Incomplete" draft was finalized on October 14, 1950, as still "Temporary" but now "Complete" (with musical numbers more or less in place).[59] These changes are itemized in table 2.1 in the next chapter. Most notably, "Tongue Twisters," the earliest version of what became "Moses," was added, along with a scene in which the writers suggest Zelda Zanders might sing "I've Got a Feelin' You're Foolin.'" Cosmo recognizes Kathy dancing in the chorus line behind Zelda and fetches Don. Many more changes were yet to come.

Satirizing the Studio

Much of the musical score for the first draft was not by Freed and Brown. In his previous film, *An American in Paris,* Kelly's best male buddy was played by Oscar Levant, a witty, brainy actor who had made a name for himself as a concert pianist and film composer, then as a panelist on a popular radio quiz show, *Information Please.*[60] Anticipating the possible casting of Levant as Cosmo Cosgrove, Comden and Green provided the character with plenty of wisecracks and piano music performed onscreen: a concerto, arrangements of Viennese waltzes and anthems, and the nineteenth-century American popular song "The Old Grey Mare," ostensibly as another jab at Lina Lamont. "It's for you, Lina," cooed Cosmo. "Have a piece of sugar."[61] The song was originally an attack on an aging Baltimore mayor running for re-election, and it doesn't seem too unkind to wonder if it was a thinly disguised reference to Freed's boss, L. B. Mayer. Note the homonyms "mare," "mayor," and "Mayer." In his late sixties (his birthdate is uncertain), Mayer retired from MGM while *Singin'* was in production.

In yet another tiny rebellion against Mayer, a poster for *Lovey Mary* (1926), another movie featuring William Haines, the star of *Excess Baggage,* appears in the film (59:09). Although he was a major star at MGM during

Table 1.2 Films within the film in the First Incomplete Draft Screenplay (musical numbers in parentheses)

[Premiere of *The Royal Rogue*]

1. Premiere of *The Royal Rogue* at the Egyptian Theatre on Hollywood Boulevard

2. Don's autobiography (Cosmo and Don sing "Fit as a Fiddle")

3. Fans attack Don and he leaps into Kathy's car to escape. Don romances Kathy; she repels him.

4. After-party at R. F.'s. Kathy, aiming at Don, hits Lina in the face with cake. (Kathy and ensemble sing "You Are My Lucky Star")

[Production and Premiere of *The Dueling Cavalier*]

5. At the studio, Don and Cosmo wait for Lina to arrive on the set. (unspecified piano number suggested)

6. Don and Lina kiss passionately for the camera while fighting bitterly about Kathy; R. F. shuts down production.

7. At the studio for their first day shooting a "talkie," Don and Cosmo encounter Kathy on her way to an audition. (duet for Don and Kathy suggested, possibly a medley of "Chant of the Jungle," "Would You," and "Broadway Melody")

8. Difficulties recording Lina on the set, ending with R. F. yanking on the wrong cord and tripping her

9. Disastrous Premiere of *The Dueling Cavalier,* with flawed soundtrack and wooden acting from Don and Lina

10. It is raining. At the Pink Fedora Restaurant, Cosmo thinks of dubbing Kathy's voice. (Two musical numbers proposed, an unspecified duet for Don and Cosmo and a trio set in "rainy streets" for Kathy, Cosmo, and Don, "Singin' in the Rain")

[Production and Premiere of *The Dancing Cavalier*]

11. R. F. approves dubbing Kathy's voice over Lina's; the film is retitled *The Dancing Cavalier*. (musical number proposed, the "Piano-Playing Pioneer")

12. While Kathy dubs lines, Don visits. Lina catches them kissing. (Kathy possibly dubs "All I Do I Dream of You"; love duet also proposed, "You Were Meant for Me")

13. Lina forces R. F. to keep Kathy's dubbing a secret.

14. Premiere of *The Dancing Cavalier* at the Egyptian Theatre. Afterward Don asks Kathy to keep on dubbing Lina without credit; Kathy breaks up with him. (two musical numbers shown onscreen including "a big finale")

15. After-party at Don's house. Lina agrees to sing if Kathy will dub her, live. Don and Cosmo expose Lina's subterfuge.

[Premiere of *Broadway Rhythm*]

16. Time has passed. Premiere of *Broadway Rhythm* starring Kathy and Don. Cosmo and Lina, now married, attend as well. ("Big musical number — finale" suggested)

Source: *Singin' in the Rain* [draft script dated August 10, 1950, with some inserted pages dated as late as September 14; marked on cover: "Temporary Incomplete"], Turner/MGM Scripts, 2642-f.1234, AL.

Figure 1.2 Lina, R. F., Don, Roscoe, and Cosmo by a cut-down poster for *Lovey Mary*.

the early sound era, Haines refused to stay as deep in the closet as Mayer required. Before he could be driven out of Hollywood as an actor, he adroitly changed professions, becoming a noted interior designer alongside his life partner Jimmie Shields. The pair were hired by many Hollywood homemakers and were still practicing in the 1950s. The woman leaping into Haines's arms in the poster is Bessie Love, who also made history at MGM as a star in *Broadway Melody* (1929), Brown and Freed's early Oscar-winning success as songwriters and the source of some of the songs in *Singin' in the Rain*, discussed in chapter 4. See figures 1.2 and 1.3.[62]

"Are You Anybody?"—Studios as Star Factories

The writers' first version of Hollywood history contained more prominent explorations of themes that were toned down in the finished film. One was the weapon Mayer wielded against Haines, Hollywood's finely tuned system for commodifying and controlling celebrities. The studios manufactured stars

Figure 1.3 The complete poster for the film *Lovey Mary* (1926).

for fans to dream about, packaging them into forgettable films. Accelerating a trend that began in the silent era, Hollywood studios created and cultivated new stars and new talent for behind-the-camera roles as well. Donald Knox put it more kindly in 1973, writing that "discovering and promoting new talent were MGM specialties."[63] The advent of sound temporarily accelerated this process by largely eliminating actors like the fictional Lina who couldn't speak (or sing) as well as they looked.

One version of Comden and Green's first draft ends with a cameo appearance by Spencer Tracy, a celebrated actor in the latter decades of his long career but still universally recognizable in 1952. He follows Don and his new co-star Kathy Selman (the last name was changed later to Sands, then finally to Selden) into the premiere of their new film, *Broadway Rhythm*. A child approaches Tracy and, not recognizing him, asks innocently, "Hey, are you anybody?"[64]

Comden and Green repeated this question no fewer than six times in their first draft. Each time the question points up both the allure and evanescence of Hollywood fame. At the silent film premiere opening the movie, three fans direct various versions of the question to Don's sidekick Cosmo, asking "Hey, who're you?," "Hey, who's this guy—I never heard of him!," and finally (in the first appearance of what becomes an interrogatory refrain), "Hey, mister, are you anybody?"[65] As mentioned, at this point Cosmo was being written for Oscar Levant, who co-starred with Kelly in *An American in Paris*. In the first draft Cosmo responds to his questioners in Levant's signature ironic mode, lamenting "that remark will send me right back to my analyst in Vienna."[66] Once Cosmo was recast with O'Connor the scene was rewritten: Cosmo was expected to make a wisecrack about being "Rin Tin Tin's stand-in," then launch into a wild imitation of a dog barking that frightened the crowd.[67] The scene disappeared from the final cut.

In the first draft as in the final film, on the way to the movie after-party, Lina asks Don why she wasn't allowed to speak for herself to her adoring fans. A stage direction reads: "We hear her voice for the first time. It is flat and coarse and a terrific shock coming out of that beautiful face." Lina tells Don and a publicity man, Rod, to write her a speech, saying "I could memoralize [sic] it." Cosmo interjects, "Sure, why don't you go out now and recite the Gettysburg Address?" She responds in her sharpest, most raucous tone of voice, "What do you know about it . . . [?] Are you anybody?"[68] This is the only instance of the "anybody" line that is retained in the final cut (13:45).

Rod takes Lina away to travel separately to the party with R. F. and his wife. Rather than Cosmo giving Don a lift as in the final cut, in the first draft screenplay both Cosmo and Don take their own cars to R. F.'s party.[69] After Don departs, Cosmo confronts himself as he passes a mirror and "looks at himself—puzzled," repeating the question, "Hey—are you anybody?"[70] Levant might have delivered this line in ironic fashion, since the mirror does reveal that he exists. He is somebody—but what Lina meant was that his opinion didn't matter. More likely, Levant might have tried to convey that Lina's putdown may have struck home. But in any case, the line disappears, replaced in the "OK" script by one of several comic parodies of Al Jolson, bathetic star of *The Jazz Singer,* written for O'Connor as Cosmo.

Much later in the first draft screenplay, as in the final print, Cosmo hatches the idea of Kathy doubling Lina's voice in order to save the remake of Don and Lina's next silent film as a talkie. R. F. promotes him to Associate Producer on the spot. On the way out from this triumphant meeting, Cosmo asks himself the question again as he passes another conveniently placed mirror, "(grinning at himself, pleased) / Hey, are you anybody?"[71] Thanks to the advent of sound movies, Cosmo is now indeed the cinematic somebody he has longed to be.

At the final film premiere in the first script, after "Mr. and Mrs. Don Lockwood [Don and Kathy]" (in some drafts, followed by Spencer Tracy) stride happily into the theater, Dora, the gossip columnist and M. C., announces: "And here come the associate producer of the film, Cosmo Cosgrove and his new wife, the former Lina Lamont. She is now appearing in 'The Jungle Princess,' in which she doesn't say a word—she just grunts!"[72] A child (perhaps the same one who accosted Tracy) then emerges from the crowd and, starry-eyed, asks Cosmo for an autograph. Cosmo hesitates, then asks the kid: "Say, are you anybody?"[73]

The prominence Comden and Green attached to this catch phrase via placement, repetition, and narrative sequence was exactly the kind of craft they might also have exercised in placing one or more of Freed and Brown's songs into their draft, using reprises to tie together the score as well as the story. But instead the writers came up with their own spoken refrain to highlight both the allure and the impermanence of film stardom. "Are you anybody?" is a tag line suitable, perhaps, for a screwball comedy, not for a musical.

When Comden and Green's refrain was minimized in the interest of streamlining the story and making room for music and dance numbers, the destruction of Lina Lamont's stardom at the film's climax became detached from the writers' larger point: stars as disposable products turned out by the star-making machinery, rather than the enduring legends most actors (and writers) hope to become. A manufactured Hollywood star is always just one flop away from eclipse. Even a star as durable as Spencer Tracy fades away with time.

The scene in which Lina describes herself as a "shimmering, glowing star in the cinema firmament," quoting from a puff piece her agent has placed in order to undermine Kathy Selden's projected future career, ends differently in the first draft.[74] There Lina suddenly reveals the careful calculation behind her veneer as a seemingly dumb blonde. After triumphing over R. F., she exultantly declares, "I'm supposed to be so dumb. So I never studied geometry but I sure know a few of the angles."[75] Despite losing some of her own designated wisecracks as the screenplay progressed, Lina is still an extraordinarily likable villain in the final cut, thanks to Jean Hagen's bravura performance.

"You've Seen One, You've Seen Them All"—Studios and Art vs. Commerce

At several points in the first screenplay draft Comden and Green addressed the tension between artistic ambition and commercial appeal inherent to popular culture. After a policeman confirms his identity and Kathy apologizes to Don for mistaking him for a carjacker, he assumes his fame will work its usual magic. He snakes his hand around Kathy's back as she drives. Kathy repels his advances by attacking his acting, saying of his movies with Lina, "If you've seen one, you've seen them all." Don, his vanity injured and his own deepest fear revealed, withdraws his arm. They proceed to argue furiously. Already disheveled by his encounter with fans who ripped his tuxedo in search of souvenirs, Don rips his coat getting out of the car, prompting a rich, ridiculing belly laugh from Kathy. Romances that began in discord were often an aspect of the screwball comedies of the 1930s and 1940s such as those teaming Katharine Hepburn with Spencer Tracy and Fred Astaire's films with Ginger Rogers.[76]

As they arrive on set to work on Don's next picture with Lina, Cosmo mischievously suggests, "why don't you just release the last one under a new title?" Then Cosmo repeats Kathy's put-down that stayed Don's wandering hands during their first meeting—"if you've seen one, you've seen them all" (26:23). These two moments are preserved in the final film. A third instance of the refrain occurs in the dialogue preceding Kathy and Don's love duet. In the first draft Kathy confesses to Don that, far from disdaining his work, she's actually seen all ten of his movies with Lina. Don replies, mocking himself, "But I still insist—'if you've seen one, you've seen them all.'"[77] In the final film the dialogue was altered into something more conversational, one of many such minor dialogue alterations that probably arose in rehearsals (40:28).

Al Jolson, the first star of the sound era, also becomes a signifier for this tension. Just as with the previous minor refrains above, the writers' references to Jolson in the first draft were juggled and reworded, in this case not only making them less significant but also less acid. In Comden and Green's first draft, Jolson's first hit talkie, *The Jazz Singer,* is retitled *Mammy's Boy.* The reference to a "Mammy" brings Jolson's now notorious blackface routine in that film immediately to mind.[78]

When R. F. announces that the studio is closing down temporarily to convert to sound because of the success of *Mammy's Boy*, Cosmo improvises a declamatory Jolsonesque song at the piano, originally with lyrics by Comden and Green based on their fictional film title. Cosmo mockingly sings "I'm Mammy's Boy—her pride and joy." Then R. F. announces that the studio will remake Lina and Don's silent picture already in progress, and Cosmo immediately adds another line: "I'm a Dueling Cavalier—and believe me I've no fear."[79] Jolson's maudlin sincerity is parodied by Cosmo, but his commercial success is openly envied by R. F.

In the "OK" screenplay *The Jazz Singer* is mentioned by name. Comden and Green rewrote the first line of their suggested lyric for Cosmo, retaining a reference to "Mammy": "Mammy! Mammy - / The sun shines east - / The sun shines west—."[80] However, in the final print of the film, O'Connor instead sings, "Oh my darling little Mammy, down in Alabammy," another of a number of instances where the cast evidently improvised their own elaborations on Comden and Green's lines (33:34).

Although these minor refrains were cut down in later script drafts, the tension between commerce and creativity remains a theme, one built up in other ways by the directors. In the "Broadway Ballet," Kelly illustrates the commercial showbiz tendency to recycle previous successes employed as a theme by Comden and Green in movement. In the ballet Don recapitulates a performer's progress toward stardom, performing the same refrain about "happy feet" as a dancing clown in the "Columbia Burlesque" house (1:22:49), at the "Palace Vaudeville" theater (1:23:05), and in the *Ziegfeld Follies* (1:23:21). The identical musical number is repackaged with differing costumes and sets to suit three different audiences. If you've seen one, you have indeed seen them all.

This commercial fare, repetitive and class conscious, is contrasted with the two extended, surrealistic pas de deux with Cyd Charisse featuring memorable props like a white wedding-style dress with a short veil and shorter hemline and an immense, enveloping train many yards long. Kelly also manufactures a punctuating refrain from the song "Broadway Rhythm," "gotta dance!" The refrain (which also appears in the number featuring the song concluding *Broadway Melody of 1936*) becomes a crucial turning point toward the end of the ballet as Don, rejected and dejected, exits the casino, then perks up as he hears a distant repetition of "gotta dance!" from another eager migrant, a younger version of himself. The result is a nostalgic rather than satirical take on the ups and downs of stardom.

Influences on Comden and Green: Previous Projects, Old Studio Movies

On the Town and *Bombshell*

Comden and Green themselves cited their first collaboration with Kelly and Donen as co-directors, *On the Town* (1949), as the immediate inspiration for their screenplay for *Singin' in the Rain*.[81] Specifically, they said they sought to scribble another "intimate movie musical in which almost all the musical numbers were handled by a small group of principals in realistic situations," as in *On the Town*.[82] Comden and Green based their screenplay on their own Broadway hit of 1944 for which they wrote both the book and the lyrics (and in which they appeared onstage in supporting roles). The stage show's score was by another young newcomer and friend, Leonard Bernstein. Kelly called the film his favorite in a 1974 interview, singling out the location shots and relatively rapid montages as "quite novel in those days" and claiming that "we took a lot of clichés out of the musical" genre in the film.[83] Most of Bernstein's music was replaced at MGM's behest with new music by their contract employee Roger Edens, although Comden and Green got to write the lyrics to these new songs.

Even when Kelly was still at work on *An American in Paris,* according to Donen he was already committed to the project: "The picture was always going to be for Gene, always."[84] Donen met with the writers while they were at work on the first draft, watching "literally dozens" of old movies with them for inspiration and possible adaptation.[85] Both he and Kelly favored the film farce *Bombshell* (1933) as a model to adapt into a musical. According to Donen, the creative quartet "considered that for a while . . . Gene and I loved it."[86] It doesn't detract from Comden and Green's claims of creating an original story to point out multiple points of similarity in another film that they did in fact study and consider as a model during their six months of labor in 1950.

Comden and Green described three initial ideas for the opening of the film, one of which is even closer to an autobiographical scene in *Bombshell*: "a magazine interview with the star in Hollywood telling a phony life story."[87] In *Bombshell*, the star Lola Burns manages to maintain a double identity: refined on the screen, beset and frazzled at home. Lina, too, is actually as vulgar and raw and real as any of her gum-chewing fans—but she can't match her voice up with her onscreen persona as an aristocratic beauty as Lola does. One can tick off several creative reuses of elements from *Bombshell*'s opening minutes in *Singin'* (with references to the time points in *Singin'* listed in parentheses): blonde star (3:16), both loyal and crazed fans held back by uniformed guards (3:30), falsified autobiography (4:25–10:50, recited by Don to a gossip columnist and her radio audience), and a monumental studio gate (7:47). Like Lola, Don is also assaulted by crazed fans who rip his clothes into souvenir swatches (15:09).

One line in the film is directly drawn from another source, the early MGM talkie *His Glorious Night* (1929), in which John Gilbert repeated the words "I love you" several times in a row (57:42). It is a standard part of any actor's training to repeat a phrase in this way, varying emphases to color and re-color the words. But this particular usage (which has been specifically cited by Comden and Green and included in their first draft completed in August 1950) has become one of the folktales of the transitional era, masking efforts by Mayer to end Gilbert's bargaining power as a major star often compared at the time to the late Rudolph Valentino.[88] Kevin Brownlow and John Kobal attributed the audience's reported laughter at this scene not to Gilbert's resonant voice but to poor direction and excessive attention to proper diction, perhaps sparked by coaches like those so roundly intoning in *Singin'* (46:35 and 47:02).[89] Comden and Green's borrowings and reshapings are not just topical but creative and effective.

Lina Lamont and Sexual Politics: Studios and Sexual Exploitation

The word "studio" with its cozy associations with artistry was a euphemism in Hollywood for describing a factory complex largely controlled by aging men. As director Amy Heckerling once put it, "Hollywood is the dream factory, and no one dreams about older women."[90] Lina Lamont, the slightly older woman Comden and Green envisioned as the central villain in *Singin' in the Rain*, is certainly re-enacting an oppressive stereotype. Lina's beauty and ambition take her far but ultimately can't hide her lack of talent. The verisimilitudes of Comden and Green's depictions of gender inequalities in Hollywood were informed by recent personal experience. Both writers were close friends with their fellow cabaret performer Judy Holliday. The opposite of the fictional Lina, Holliday had to get producers to look past her beauty to her tremendous talents as an actor.

As a fellow founding member of the cabaret quintet The Revuers, Judy Holliday had arrived with Comden and Green in Hollywood in 1944, booked to appear in a film tentatively titled *Duffy's Tavern*. By the time they arrived the film had been canceled. Their agent at the time, Kurt Frings, booked the group into a nightclub, the Trocadero, instead. The group pursued further auditions. Twentieth Century-Fox studios wanted to sign only Judy. Much later "I told Sidney [Lumet] some of the feelings I had as the other girl in the group [underline in original]," recalled Comden in an unpublished 1981 memoir.[91]

Holliday signed with Fox but only on the condition that the entire quintet would be hired to appear in at least one picture. This ended up being a period piece set in the 1920s, *Greenwich Village* (1944, starring Carmen Miranda). "Originally we had two numbers to do, our own 'Baroness Bazooka' and part of something written for the picture called 'It's All for Art's Sake'," recalled Comden.[92]

Holliday was successfully plucked from the group for grooming as a star, against her will. "We all had an apartment together. . . . It wasn't too happy to be unemployed and unwanted and living with one who was both working and wanted although miserable," summed up Comden.[93]

Holliday's career at Fox fizzled following a film appearance in a minor role in *Winged Victory* (1944). But her Broadway career took off in 1946 when she created the role of Billie Dawn in the drama *Born Yesterday*. She returned to Hollywood in 1949 for a supporting role in the screwball comedy *Adam's Rib* starring Katharine Hepburn and Spencer Tracy. Only then was she approached about recreating the role of Billie Dawn by a different studio, Columbia. Holliday won an Oscar for her bravura performance using multiple vocal timbres as the abused wife of a war profiteer in the 1950 film version of *Born Yesterday*.[94]

Lina's voice may certainly have been inspired in part by Holliday's performance. Pratibha Dabholkar and Earl Hess judiciously describe Hagen's characterization of Lina as "related" to Holliday's performances as Billie Dawn but "not a duplication."[95] Hagen paid back the debt with interest, creating her own amalgam of differing voices along a more limited expressive spectrum, never letting even her most honeyed tones veer too closely to the quiet end of Holliday's soft wistful voice with its pronounced Queens, New York, lilt.[96]

However, late in life Freed cited a different model for Lina. "She was a composite of a lot of silent stars ... Mae Murray was exactly it."[97]

Lina's patois and her big-city stridency were keys to her character (although in fact Hagen was raised in Indiana, not Queens). There is something admirable in Lina's refusal to be ashamed of her way of speaking. By the mid-1930s in the depths of the Great Depression, many Hollywood stars like Jean Harlow and Joan Crawford played roles that required them to speak in ways that signified a working-class or rural background. Lina's refusal to compromise her own roots becomes a problem only because she has been typecast in a series of silent films as an aristocrat.

Self-Reflexivity or Irreverent Nostalgia?

Many previous writers including Jane Feuer have explored self-reflexivity in *Singin'*.[98] Other films have self-reflexive moments; *Singin'* is full of them. To put a theoretical concept into everyday language, Comden and Green not only drew upon earlier musical films as sources ("conservative self-reflexivity" in Feuer's terms), they had their characters comment on the medium—"critical self-reflexivity."[99] Let a single example stand for the whole here. In the first draft as in the finished film, after listening to the disgruntled audience at a disastrous preview of his first sound film Don realizes that his good looks don't compensate for his wooden acting. Forced to confront his own limits, he announces to his friends Cosmo and Kathy that, once *The Dueling Cavalier* opens, "Lockwood and Lamont are a museum piece." Just as museum curators choose stories to tell about intriguing objects in order to engage visitors, Comden and Green get viewers hooked on a history lesson, not least by letting their characters worry about fading into the past themselves.

Don's personal crisis throws the emphasis on looks rather than talent in Hollywood more generally into sharp relief. Beauty sells. Lina's failings are many, but her power to make money for the studio is undeniable. The studio itself, late to the talkie party, is on the line. Monumental Pictures, too, may become history. Everyone in the cast and crew knew that MGM might soon suffer the same fate. Self-reflexivity can trigger deep nostalgia, perhaps another reason *Singin'* kept rising in critics' and fans' esteem as the years passed and the old studio system faded away.

Self-reflexivity is not the only useful theoretical frame for this "movie about the movies." Even Comden and Green's original first draft satires are imbued with an irreverent nostalgia. The writers were celebrating the shortcomings of an era when movie-making was a far more creative business in many ways. In the oppressive atmosphere of the blacklists and the Cold War, the 1920s may have looked something like what the 1960s have come to signify in our own time: an era of loosening mores, modernizing media, and aesthetic experimentation. Interpreting the film's references to filmmaking as both nostalgic homage and aesthetic critique ("no, no, no!") offers a way to appreciate both the self-reflexive forms and the substantive social critiques within the film. *Singin'* doesn't uncritically celebrate Hollywood; it recreates an era of transformation in American filmmaking, a more creative moment. But the film's version of Hollywood is indeed a company town, softened most decisively by R. F.'s fictional enlightened despotism and the plot's focus: not on the evils of the system, but on the hilarious malice of an antiheroine with a tragic sonic flaw.

2

Revising the Screenplay

"Gene Kelly bristles with ideas for his pictures. He is like a race horse. You have to hold him back, or he'll run away with the whole setup."

Arthur Freed in the *Los Angeles Times* (1951)

Comden and Green's first draft, completed in October 1950, provided a strong, coherent narrative, but problems remained, including how to end the film. Comden and Green's ideas for musical numbers were provisional, with many shaped to fit Oscar Levant's particular strengths and weaknesses. Sometimes the writers suggested where to place a number without specifying what song they had in mind. One of these suggestions was the finale, although one might reasonably assume that this might include a reprise of "Singin' in the Rain."

Exactly how to end the film remained an unresolved issue even after production began in the spring and summer of 1951. After Comden and Green left *Singin'* in the hands of the directors and returned to New York in mid-April, a ghost writer was brought in during production. Although his contribution wasn't used, Joseph Fields drafted an alternative finale dated July 26, 1951, in which Kelly swings on ropes backstage and battles a stagehand for control of the stage curtain in order to expose Lina.[1] At some point the creative team came up with a solution: the movie ends with a flash forward to a billboard advertising yet another film, this time starring Don and Kathy, titled (in the final cut) *Singin' in the Rain*. This scene was settled on so late in production that apparently no revised pages describing it were generated; the first written description of the final version of the film's ending appears in the continuity script, a transcript of the final cut.

Generally, revisions were printed up and inserted in copies of both major working drafts of the screenplay listed in table 1.1. Some of these changes blunted the satire in Comden and Green's early drafts; others improved upon promising material, such as the addition of Don's supposed family motto, "Dignity, always dignity" (4:35).[2] His words are underscored in the final

Singin' in the Rain. Andrew Buchman, Oxford University Press. © Oxford University Press 2024.
DOI: 10.1093/9780197760062.003.0002

print with composer/arranger Conrad Salinger's distinctive music, played softly by a string quartet.[3]

During 1951 before and during production the expressive weight of the film shifted decisively toward a series of musical numbers devised by Kelly and Donen. By 1951, Donen, just twenty-seven, had already worked with Kelly on five major Hollywood productions: *Cover Girl* (1944, at Columbia), *Anchors Aweigh* (1945), *Living in a Big Way* (1947), *Take Me Out to the Ball Game* (1949), and *On the Town* (1949).[4] The co-directors reused many of the same songs Comden and Green had suggested using in the first draft but moved them to different places in the script, sometimes changing the performers around as well. Casting changes played a major role, particularly the replacement of Oscar Levant with a gifted young dancer borrowed at considerable expense from another studio, Donald O'Connor. O'Connor was performing regularly on the new mass medium of the moment, television, but was contractually tied to Universal Studios, stuck in a series of profitable but sophomoric films co-starring Francis, "the talking mule."[5]

Daily A. D. (Assistant Director) Reports in the Freed Papers preserved at the University of Southern California's Cinematic Library provide a detailed chronology of specific shots day by day, but they do not record Kelly and Donen's creative decisions. Before and during production, the directors consulted with Comden and Green in person or on the phone. Comden and Green said their script conferences with Kelly and Donen generally involved "structure" rather than "specific lines." "If they were going to change a number—put one number in instead of another—then of course there'd have to be a different lead-in to the scene."[6] But as already mentioned in chapter 1, these changes were sometimes tweaked further in rehearsals during production, then documented after the fact in the final Continuity Script, a working document produced in-house for use by technicians.[7]

Smaller issues like choosing between camera angles and takes were undertaken with the assistance of veteran cinematographer Hal Rosson and film editor Adrienne Fazan. Apparently, Kelly typically directed the actors in rehearsals and on the set, with Donen remaining behind the camera. "Every move, he [Kelly] knew exactly what he wanted," recalled Reynolds in 2002.[8] In the editing suite during post-production Donen came into his own. As Donen put it himself late in life, "In a movie [during the editing phase] I just do what I want and everybody finds out about it later."[9]

Some changes necessitated negotiations with Freed and other executives. Hugh Fordin's budget figures are widely cited, but unfortunately not sourced, so must be taken with a grain of salt.[10] According to Fordin, Kelly asked for and received an additional $520,000 ($6.2 million in 2024 dollars) to cover an ambitious, lengthy dream ballet comparable to that in *An American in Paris*, making the first cut of the picture about two hours long.[11] Both the film's ending and the penultimate ballet took shape as the production itself progressed. Despite the additional allocation, Fordin states that the film went over budget by about 25 percent, costing $2,540,800, $620,996 over the augmented budget. Fortunately this story had a happy ending (again, according to Fordin); the film ended up grossing $7,665,000 during its first release in movie theaters (including international receipts).[12]

The quote at the head of this chapter comparing Kelly to "a race horse" (one of L. B. Mayer's favorite hobbies) is a comment from Freed in a profile that appeared on April 15, 1951, the same week Freed gave his "OK" to the revised screenplay.[13] In short order Comden and Green departed, leaving Kelly and Donen with a screenplay approved by Freed for production but still rough at the edges. Ironically, the writers' willingness to entrust their manuscript to the co-directors whom they esteemed as friends and colleagues became the crux of Donen's protests around what he considered to be Comden and Green's exaggerated claims to authorship, discussed below.

Questions of Authorship

Most writers have concluded that the musical numbers, and many of the lesser cuts and adjustments devised by Kelly and Donen, made *Singin'* a much better film (with the exception of the ballet), and that judgment seems sound given both the film's immediate popularity and its rising and lasting reputation since. But one can still wonder if Comden and Green's original, more scathing portrait of Hollywood as a factory, manufacturing disposable stars and repetitive (but popular) moving pictures, might have been preserved as well. One factor in the change of direction may have been Billy Wilder's film noir *Sunset Boulevard*, which had tilled similar territory successfully the previous year, garnering nominations for eleven Oscars.[14] Another biting satire of Hollywood might have been shunned by critics and audiences alike as not as good as last year's model movie.

Some critiques of the film industry from the first draft screenplay did survive. "If you've seen one, you've seen them all," Comden and Green's dismissal of Hollywood products in general, remained in the screenplay from first draft to final print.[15] But the boss, producer/lyricist Freed, provided a riposte in a song composed during production in response to a request from Kelly for a solo for O'Connor. In "Make 'Em Laugh," the one new song Freed and Brown contributed, there's a contradictory line that rings just as true: "you can charm the critics and have nothing to eat" (28:03).[16] Comden, Green, and Freed disagreed on where, exactly, popular culture and artistic ambitions can coincide.

"Could We Do Better?"—Kelly and Donen as Screenplay Editors

Before returning to California to help revise the screenplay for *Singin'*, Comden and Green worried that they might be required to devote more time to the project. They knew that a clause in their contract specified that they were not to leave the studio until both Freed and his boss, Dore Schary (who had largely displaced Mayer as head of production beginning in 1948), were satisfied with the revised script.[17] Eager to get back to work on their new Broadway revue, they asked their new agent, Irving "Swifty" Lazar, to make it clear to Freed that they could not prolong their stay beyond three weeks.[18] Comden and Green indeed spent only three more weeks on salary between March 26 and April 14, 1951, meeting often with Kelly at his home in the evenings off the record. As mentioned in chapter 1 Kelly was still on mandatory unpaid leave after finishing work on *An American in Paris*.[19] It is likely that Donen was also present. According to Betsy Blair, "Although he [Donen] had an apartment of his own, he practically lived with us, so much so that George Cukor once asked 'who is that young man who's always asleep on your floor?' "[20]

Once Freed signed off on the "OK" script on April 11, Kelly and Donen appear to have taken over much of the rewriting, which continued throughout rehearsals and shooting days. In their introduction to the published script Comden and Green assert authorship of only one scene after delivering the "OK" screenplay: the dialogue leading into Kathy and Don's slow dance to "You Were Meant for Me." This new number replaced a previously planned medley of songs. In Philadelphia for tryouts of *Two on the Aisle*, "we wrenched our minds away from the great Bert Lahr just two blocks away," the writers recalled, "and time-machined ourselves back into *Singin' in the Rain* long enough to fill the order."[21]

Donen vehemently claimed a major editorial role in an interview with a curator from the Museum of Modern Art in 1974. "Mostly it's a lot of lies, what they're saying in their preface [to the edition of the *Singin' in the Rain* screenplay published in 1972]. It isn't true, none of it is true. Adolph is saying that they went off and wrote that script and then sent it to Gene and that Gene then said he would do it. The total opposite is true; we all met for weeks in California and talked about it. Gene was going to be in it, they were writing a part for him. It's not at all what they've said. I don't care really, but it's peculiar."[22]

Donen also made his case in an interview with biographer Joseph Casper: "Gene and I loved it [i.e., Comden and Green's first draft of a screenplay]. Whatever thoughts we had for additions or deletions were incorporated into the script. The [1972] published Rain script is the script taken off the screen after all our changes before and even during the production . . . not the script Betty and Adolph gave us. [Betty and] Adolph's Foreword in the [1972] book is incorrect."[23] In that book Comden and Green do credit Kelly and Donen for both "the musical numbers" and the "montages" in the film in a prefatory note.[24] In support of Donen's most pointed criticism, the composite script preserved by Comden and Green certainly suggests that the 1972 published version of the script was based on pages from previous drafts, plus new transcriptions of dialogue and scene directions transcribed directly from the film itself.[25]

Donen's involvement in the project certainly stretched from story conferences with Comden and Green in the late spring and summer of 1950 involving models like *Bombshell*, discussed in chapter 1, through intensive post-production editing work that continued into early 1952. Donen collaborated with two relatively unsung women who contributed substantially to the final cut, veteran film editor Adrienne Fazan and uncredited sound supervisor Lela Simone. Simone's work is addressed in chapter 4.

Donen's protests suggest that the co-directors had more to do with the creation of even the first draft of the script than Comden and Green acknowledged; his differing account of work on the script in 1950 warrants further investigation if and when Kelly and Donen's personal papers become more accessible to researchers.[26] But it is clear just by comparing the "OK" draft to the finished film that the co-directors continued editing, as Comden and Green repeatedly acknowledged.

Although Kelly's working copy of the screenplay was lost in a house fire, working scripts of other films housed among Kelly's papers at Boston

University give a sense of how methodically Kelly prepared, especially when he was directing.[27] For example, in his working copy of the screenplay for *The Happy Road* (1957), a Franco-American comedy that he directed and in which he also starred, tabbed divider pages were inserted to separate the script into scenes. Extensive handwritten notations on almost every page suggested not just approaches to lines but numerous ideas for changes in lines and stage directions. Another strategy Kelly adopted was simply to question specific lines, asking the writers, "could we do better?"[28]

Pages inserted into copies of the working "OK" script of *Singin'* week by week document some but not all of Kelly and Donen's changes, hand-stitching musical numbers and improving the flow of scenes incorporating dialogue and action. Kelly and Donen sought to achieve a standard of integration closer to the Broadway norm but in a Hollywood production in progress. It's probable that the directors were assisted at rehearsals and on the set by clerical staff (including script supervisor Dorothy Aldrin) who made note of changes and took care of script updates for them.[29]

Table 2.1 summarizes Comden and Green's suggestions for musical numbers in their first drafts of the screenplay. Table 2.2 summarizes the numbers in the finished film. Since there was no final version of a shooting script, film timings are substituted for page numbers in this second table. With the exception of "Chant of the Jungle," which was cut, as mentioned many of the songs the writers suggested at various points in the first draft were retained but moved around and placed into different contexts in the story. Additional old songs by Freed and Brown were also added; these appear with the dates of their first appearance in a previous film in table 2.2.

Almost all of the music by other composers (much of it intended for performance by Oscar Levant on piano) disappeared entirely. Two new songs were added: "Make 'Em Laugh" (newly composed for *Singin'*, credited to Freed and Brown), and "Moses" (with lyrics by Comden and Green and music by Edens).[30] "Moses" realized a suggestion Comden and Green made in their first draft, "Possibly this whole diction section may be handled musically."[31] Edens also wrote music and lyrics for a new verse section for Reynolds's solo performance of Brown and Freed's song "You Are My Lucky Star," at least some of the lead-in patter concerning long and short faces recited by O'Connor for the song "Make 'Em Laugh," and the narration for the "Beautiful Girl" fashion show interpolated into Comden and Green's script.[32]

Table 2.1 Musical Numbers in the First Draft Screenplay

Title	Sung by	on page
"Fit as a Fiddle" (1932, Freed, Hoffman, Goodhart)	Don & Cosmo	5
piano and violin mood music	Don & Cosmo (play)	7
"Fit as a Fiddle" reprise on piano	Cosmo (on piano)	9
Tschaikowsky "Romeo and Juliet" overture	~~Cosmo (on piano)~~	12
party music (unspecified)	background at mansion	24
"You Are My Lucky Star" (1935)	Kathy	29
"improvising"	**Cosmo**	**32**
~~Paderewski Minuet~~	~~Cosmo (on piano)~~	~~33~~
~~"NUMBER - PIANO SELECTION (unspecified)~~	~~Cosmo (on piano)~~	~~33~~
unspecified musical number	**Cosmo and Don**	35
"Old Grey Mare She Ain't What She Used to Be"	Cosmo (on piano)	~~34~~ **36**
theme from Tchaikowsky's "Romeo and Juliet"	Cosmo (on piano)	~~36~~ **38**
Austrian National Hymn	Cosmo (on piano)	~~38~~ **40**
"Mammy's Boy" (lyrics by Comden & Green)	Cosmo (sings & plays)	~~39~~ **41**
"I'm a Dueling Cavalier" (lyrics by Comden & Green)	Cosmo (sings & plays)	~~39~~ **41**
tongue twisters "may be handled musically" ["Moses"]	**Don**	**44**
"I've Got a Feeling You're Foolin'" (1935)	**Zelda Zonk & ensemble**	**44**
song (audition for R. F.)	**Kathy**	**46**
"Chant of the Jungle" (1929) / **"Would You?"** (1936) / **"Broadway Melody"** (1929)	Don & Kathy	~~48~~ **50**
"Romeo and Juliet" reprise [in *The Dueling Cavalier*]	**underscoring**	**55**
Musical Number (unspecified)	Don & Cosmo~~62~~	63
"Singing in the Rain" (1929)	Kathy, Don, & Cosmo~~65~~	67
"[unspecified] famous piano concerto" [in *Piano-playing Pioneer*]	Cosmo (on piano)	~~69~~ **70**
"All I Do Is Dream of You" (1929)	Kathy (dubbing Lina)	~~70~~ **71**
"You Were Meant for Me" (1929)	Kathy & Don	~~74~~ **75**
Unspecified musical number [in *The Dancing Cavalier*]	movie within movie	~~78~~ **80**
~~unspecified~~ **"Singing in the Rain"**	Kathy singing for Lina live	87
Big Musical Number - Finale (unspecified)		~~88~~ **91**

Numbers in August 10, 1950, script in plain text. Additions to October 10, 1950, script in **boldface**; deletions ~~struck through~~. Full musical numbers highlighted in grey. Brief diegetic musical passages are included. All songs by Brown and Freed unless otherwise specified; dates for songs are dates of publication.

Sources: *Singin' in the Rain* [draft script dated August 10, 1950, with some inserted pages dated as late as September 14; marked on cover: "Temporary Incomplete"], Turner/MGM Scripts, Folder 2642-f.1234, AL; and "1950-10-14 Temporary Complete Script" [draft script dated October 14, 1950, stamped on cover: "Temporary Complete"], Comden and Green Papers, Box 9, Folder 6, NYPL.

take on a major film role than Kelly's partner in *An American in Paris,* Leslie Caron, who although she had extensive ballet training had never appeared in a film before.[43] However, Reynolds, too, was still a teenager, twenty years younger than Kelly. In her narration for a documentary about the making of the film she frankly described Mayer's decision to put her into *Singin'* as "typecasting, plain and simple. They didn't want someone to *act* the part. I *was* that young, inexperienced girl you see on the screen" (her emphases).[44]

Hedda Hopper announced that "cute Debbie Reynolds will play opposite Gene Kelly in 'Singin' in the Rain'" in her nationally syndicated column in the *Los Angeles Times* on October 16, 1950.[45] Comden and Green's claim that Kelly had not committed himself to the project until January 1951 when he finished shooting *An American in Paris* appears to be an incomplete account of Kelly's involvement, even if it didn't seem guaranteed to Comden and Green.[46] An announcement that Kelly would not only star but co-direct the film with Donen didn't appear in the *Los Angeles Times* until March 3, 1951.[47]

Hopper's columns included predictions that didn't pan out, as in her announcement on April 3, 1951, that it "looks as though Gene Kelly will get Nina Foch as his co-star in 'Singin' in the Rain.'"[48] According to Fordin, Foch "was screen tested but was found not true to type."[49] Dabholkar and Hess report that Comden and Green wanted Judy Holliday to get the part.[50] Kelly also said that Holliday was the model for the character but couldn't remember if she had ever actually been approached by the studio.[51] Like O'Connor, Holliday was under contract with a competing studio (Columbia) at the time, which would entail a "lending" fee for MGM in addition to a salary appropriate for a recent "Best Actress" Oscar winner. Holliday did star in a comedy that opened, like *Singin'*, in April 1952, *The Marrying Kind,* directed by George Cukor—released by Columbia.[52]

Around ten actors were given screen tests for the part.[53] L. B. Mayer's wife, Lorena, favored Hagen.[54] Later, Kelly said that only Hagen was both "pretty enough to be believed as a movie star" and "funny enough."[55] "I just told Jean to act Judy acting Billie Dawn in *Born Yesterday*—and it was easy after that," Kelly told biographer Clive Hirschhorn.[56]

Freed was still the boss; Reynolds was not the only casting decision imposed upon Kelly. He had two full-time dance assistants, Jeanne Coyne and Carol Haney. Among other duties, they trained and rehearsed Reynolds for two months before shooting began and acted as secretaries for O'Connor, recording his improvised choreography for "Make 'Em Laugh" in the dance studio as he created it.[57] Kelly created the vamp role Cyd Charisse played in the "Broadway Ballet" with Haney in mind. According to Charisse, Kelly also wanted Haney to play the role onscreen but was overruled by Freed.[58] Charisse sometimes towers over Kelly in their two duets in the ballet, an effect he disguises by visibly crouching in her presence (1:21:18 and 1:25:13).

Kelly got two of his big asks, O'Connor as Cosmo and additional funding for a ballet. Freed and Mayer cast Reynolds, Hagen, and Charisse. As explored in chapter 1, since all three had already signed long-term contracts with MGM, their comparatively low salaries may have balanced out the high costs for a dancing Cosmo and a vast dance sequence comparable to that in *An American in Paris*. Millard Mitchell, while employed at a somewhat higher salary, was also a hard-working and productive contract player.

Sadly, Rita Moreno, cast as Lina's pal Zelda Zanders, didn't get the chance to sing or dance in the final cut, and her contract was cancelled by MGM shortly thereafter—in retrospect, missed opportunities, to say the least.[59] See figure 2.1 from one of Moreno's remaining brief appearances. Zelda leads her pal Lina to the looping booth where they surprise Don and Kathy in (mild)

Figure 2.1 Rita Moreno as Lina's pal Zelda Zanders.

flagrante delicto (1.29.57). Moreno went on to a long, illustrious career in films, television, and theater, co-starring in the film versions of *The King and I* (as Tuptim) in 1956 and of *West Side Story* (as Anita) in 1961. She also appeared in the 2021 remake of *West Side Story,* playing the kindly drugstore owner Valentina, a regendered version of the character Doc.[60]

Integrating Musical Numbers into the Narrative

As early reviewers discerned (see chapter 5), deep narrative integration in which "music, songs, and dance *become* the mode of storytelling" as employed in some other backstage musicals is not the rule in *Singin'*.[61] In the *New York Times* Bosley Crowther speculated that the film's "plot, if that's what you'd call it," was "tossed off" by Comden and Green, although at times it reached "the level of first-class satiric burlesque."[62] Instead the viewer is typically given a topical pretext for a number via a bit of introductory dialogue. However, as we'll also see in chapter 3, Kelly and Donen thought long and hard about crafting musical numbers that fit into the overall narrative logically, even if they don't explicitly move the story forward.

The opening credit sequence illustrates one of Kelly's favored modes of mechanistic integration, employing an image from the song's lyrics. The trio performs "Singing in the Rain," simultaneously acting out the song's title by singing in raincoats wielding umbrellas in a simulated rainstorm, echoing the staging of the song in *The Hollywood Revue of 1929* as performed by Cliff Edwards, then by the three Brox Sisters who share a single triple-wide transparent raincoat.

The directors were also adept at mixing up diegetic and nondiegetic elements, something the music department at MGM often aided by easing the transition into a musical number via some unobtrusive underscoring. The next four numbers are all diegetic, leading the viewer via naturalistic segues into and out of the songs and dances. This makes the inevitable shock when singing and dancing take over the screen less jarring.

"Fit as a Fiddle" and "All I Do Is Dream of You" are clearly diegetic, that is, stage performances depicted onscreen. Cosmo's big solo, "Make 'Em Laugh," begins as a diegetic attempt to cheer Don up before he starts work on his next repetitive film with dreary Lina but quickly becomes a unique fantasy with nondiegetic musical accompaniment, one of the three longest numbers in the film. The narrative trick here is believing that Cosmo would spontaneously perform not a tiny jig but a whole number. Jane Feuer has dubbed this mode "the myth of spontaneity."[63]

Feuer also observed that "spontaneous talent distinguishes Don, Cosmo, and Kathy from Lina Lamont," and that Kelly's characteristic employment of props in his choreography, which Feuer calls "bricolage," also contributes to an impression of spontaneity in his work.[64] Kelly's idea spread, becoming a trope of "the post-Gene Kelly MGM musical."[65] Within the number Cosmo directly addresses the camera, looking through the lens right into the viewer's eyes, another technique Feuer analyzes perceptively, contrasting the ways it is used to create audience engagement in Hollywood musicals with the ways it is employed as a way to break into the ongoing narrative in Brecht's plays and Jean-Luc Godard's art films.[66]

In the case of "Beautiful Girl," another number employing direct address, the casting for the lead singer was changed in order to strengthen integration into the narrative. The extended number is in ternary form, framing elaborate montages underscored with an equally elaborate medley alternating bits from Brown and Freed hits with diegetic iterations of the song by a singer in a straw hat, played in the final cut by Jimmy Thompson, a protégé of Kelly's, backed by a chorus line.[67] This ensemble is ostensibly a part of Zelda Zanders's new musical also in production as the studio converts to sound. Dabholkar and Hess observe that since Kelly made an audio recording of this number, he probably was considering performing the number himself, in character as Don Lockwood.[68] But if Don had performed in the number, he certainly would have recognized Kathy.

In the August 31, 1950, version of the first draft screenplay Comden and Green had suggested that Don and Cosmo recognize Kathy earlier in the story, among a group of dancers heading to an audition for chorus line spots at Monumental Pictures and then urge a casting director to hire her. By October 10 they had revised this scene, having Zelda Zanders perform "I've Got a Feelin' You're Foolin'" with Kathy emerging from the chorus, then auditioning for R. F. because the dance director, Sid Phillips, wants to give her a bigger part.[69] This way Kathy's promotion to a supporting role is also advocated by an unbiased part, Sid Phillips, the dance director of Zelda's musical (played by Tommy Farrell), rather by Don as in the first draft screenplay. In the "OK" script Zelda is replaced with an "innocuous juvenile lead" singing "Beautiful Girl," with Kathy in the group performing behind him. Only then do Don and Cosmo just happen to walk by and recognize Kathy (38:44); the nickel simultaneously drops for Zelda, now just seated nearby.

The next four numbers are nondiegetic, but the lines between veristic action and depicted performance are blurred. For "You Were Meant for Me" Don sets the scene as if it were a diegetic performance, complete with lights and props. But the orchestra enters from nowhere as Don begins to sing, and the number becomes a love duet integrated into the story, enacting the couple's kindling romance. "Moses" is a classic example of "the myth of spontaneity," the kind of fantastic release from schoolroom bondage that students of all ages dream about on occasion. Cosmo makes funny faces and, together with Don, they begin chanting tongue twisters in rhythm, then break into song and dance. "Good Morning" is introduced with only perfunctory dialogue, but it also expresses the jubilation the trio feels at coming up with a way to salvage *The Dueling Cavalier*: by making it into a musical. At the number's end, Cosmo embroiders this idea by figuring out a way to disguise Lina's voice as well.

"Singin' in the Rain" may seem to come out of nowhere. But the situation is appropriate to some aestheticized expression of Don's jubilation. The number certainly expresses Don's pleasure in Kathy's company. But it is also an externalization of the profound existential relief he must be feeling as well. His friends have figured out a way to save his career and keep him from becoming a museum piece.

Later numbers also blur the lines between diegetic and nondiegetic. Both "Would You?" and Kathy (and Lina's) reprise of "Singin' in the Rain" serve to illustrate the artifices behind the making of sound films, merging quasi-documentary footage with the magical cinematic illusions achieved via overdubbing. Don's appeal to Kathy, "You Are My Lucky Star," simultaneously fulfills the audience's expressed wish for a song left incomplete by Lina's discomfiture and serves to signal to Kathy that Don's feelings for her are unchanged, despite his apparent betrayal minutes earlier, meant to trick Lina into lip-synching onstage. As Vincent Canby put it in 1975, "*Singin' in the Rain* is integrated, but it's not all that integrated."[70]

Brevity is another trait common to the musical numbers in *Singin'*. Each of these closing musical numbers is less than two minutes long. The exception, of course, is the gigantic "Broadway Ballet," which remains the problem piece in *Singin'* for many critics and receives special attention in chapter 3. The entire ballet is famously justified by a few words from Don at the start, "It's the story of a young hoofer" (1:15:26), and a gag line for R. F. after we've seen the whole thing, "I can't quite visualize it" (1:28:50). This antithesis of believable integration, if believably primitive for an early talkie being salvaged in the late 1920s, isn't that far from the mechanistic modes of integration generally employed elsewhere in the film.

Transformations of Comden and Green's Ideas

Integration is sometimes held up as an ideal in the post–Rodgers and Hammerstein stage or film musical. The stellar reputation *Singin' in the Rain* has achieved without it is evidence that more modest modes of integration, combined with excellent performances and production, can more than suffice. However, a closer look at how Kelly and Donen, in collaboration with Comden and Green, arrived at "Good Morning," "You Were Meant for Me," and the "Beautiful Girl" medley (unfortunately replacing Rita Moreno's one projected number, "I've Got a Feelin' You're Foolin'") and also revised even the writers' well-formulated setup for "Fit as a Fiddle" reveals that the co-directors did think carefully about what *kind* of numbers would fit most neatly into the narrative arc of the film as a whole. To put it another way, Kelly and Donen didn't approach the issue of integration as writers; they approached it as choreographers and cinematic scene makers.

Some of Comden and Green's ideas for the musical numbers seem to have inspired Kelly and Donen to ask themselves, "could *we* do better?" As a result, the writers' ideas emerged in different forms elsewhere in the film. For example, Comden and Green's prescription for "Singing in the Rain" was a joyful trio. Peter Wollen has suggested "Make Way for Tomorrow," a trio Kelly choreographed for one of his earlier successes, *Cover Girl* (1944), as a model that may have influenced the writers.[71] In that film, Kelly, Rita Hayworth, and Phil Silvers dance down a city street together, encountering a streetlamp and a threatening policeman while singing a song with references to rain in the lyrics.[72] Kelly improved Comden and Green's plan for "Singin' in the Rain" by radically simplifying it into his own climactic solo. Similarly, Kelly's version of "You Were Meant for Me" distills Comden and Green's original idea of the couple romancing while moving between indoor film stages and performing a medley of old songs down to a Shakespearian balcony scene using a stepladder, lights, and a wind machine.

Kelly did reuse the idea of compiling a series of vignettes built around props and costumes employed in "Make Way for Tomorrow," not for the title song in *Singin'* as Comden and Green suggested but in "Good Morning."

This number is also a trio, at the same point in the plot, when Cosmo thinks up a way to make lemonade out of their lemon of a talkie. The dancers enact style vignettes, employing raincoats as can-can skirts, headless and hand-less dummies, touristic Hawai'ian muumuus and ukuleles, and toreador capes. Finally, O'Connor doffs his drag turban-like cloche (borrowed from Kathy) and recalls his aggressive dances with a dummy in "Make 'Em Laugh" and with a hapless Bobby Watson in "Moses," doing the Charleston with his raincoat as a partner before flinging the garment to the floor and kicking it across the room. Placing the trio indoors makes even more props and sets available, including an elegant wet bar repurposed as a ballet barre and not one but two climactic couches, leaped over, then tipped over by the dancers, who charge toward the camera before collapsing backward in a heap. This number is explored further in chapter 4.

Comden and Green's idea of cramming fragments from a series of Freed and Brown hits into a medley was also eventually employed in the "Beautiful Girl" sequence planned out in the "OK" script. The seed of this complex montage in the first draft screenplay was a simple series of headlines in issues of *Variety* extolling the rise of talkies, which in the finished film introduces a much more ambitious medley of musical numbers evoking Hollywood styles of the 1930s, climaxing with an elaborate fashion show and an overhead shot of a circular array of dancers employing the kaleidoscopic approach associated with choreographer/director Busby Berkeley. Kelly worked with Berkeley on *For Me and My Gal* (1942, his first film appearance) and *Take Me Out to the Ball Game* (1949). Hirschhorn suggests that the character of director Roscoe Dexter was also inspired by Berkeley.[73] We'll return to this number in chapter 3.

Finally, Kelly and Donen did adopt Comden and Green's idea for sliding "Fit as a Fiddle" into Don's autobiography on the red carpet relatively intact. The song functions as a diegetic illustration of Kelly's hard knocks in vaude-ville, contradicted in his counterfactual voiceover narrative. But a com-parison of the first draft and the "OK" script with the finished film reveals a considerable amount of could-we-do-better revision, some of it specifi-cally cinematic and some of it felicitously musical. The signage Comden and Green devised for the "OK" script, described only as a "montage" of road signs, is turned into a tightly edited series of dissolves and superimposed shots. From the moment warm strings enter to underscore Don's first reci-tation of the family motto "dignity, always dignity" (4:39) to the beginning of the musical number (5:56), ten different shots, most employing camera dollies in and out to keep the viewer's eye on relevant details, are presented in sequence.

The last ten seconds of the montage combine four shots. Don and Cosmo, in matching green and white checked suits, hats, and shoes, repeat a riff on piano and violin we've already heard in a previous barroom quartet scene. Superimposed on the pair, another camera floats over small town street signs. We infer that Cosmo and Don have toured through Dead Man's Fang, Arizona; Oatmeal, Nebraska; and Coyoteville, New Mexico (5:49–5:56).[74] These ingeniously insulting names scream "Comden and Green" and first appear in their "OK" script.

The duo onstage launches directly into "Fit as a Fiddle"—the riffs they've been playing turn into a perfect vamp-till-ready in the right key (5:56). The number is set on the lip of a stage in front of a painted backdrop of a landscape that includes a billboard for a local eatery, the "People's Grill." Here and elsewhere the scenic team, led by Cedric Gibbons, complemented Comden and Green's penchant for signage with invented signs of their own. During the era of the Hollywood blacklist, creating a restaurant called the "People's Grill" may have been a small protest by a union scene painter.

This montage replaced the scene Comden and Green had devised in the first draft, set at a "cheap vaudeville house," dramatizing Don and Cosmo's hard life on the road. A Hollywood talent scout drops in, to Don's excitement. But the scout is only interested in the canine act on the bill, known as Rip van Rip (a mashup of the Hollywood dog star Rin Tin Tin's name with that of the title character in Washington Irving's 1819 short story "Rip Van Winkle").[75]

Finding an Ending: Satire vs. Romance

As noted in table 1.1, Joseph Fields was hired to write an alternative version of the ending while the film was in production and Comden and Green were back in New York. Fields elaborated on some of Comden and Green's ideas, adding more swashbuckling for Don, but his version was not adopted.[76] The writers had suggested a musical finale without noting any specific songs for inclusion. The satirical second film premiere featuring an anonymous Spencer Tracy and revealing that Cosmo and Lina have married was dropped from the "OK" script. The previous shot sequence becomes the closing scene, with Cosmo joining Kathy and Don onstage singing a trio version of "You Are My Lucky Star."[77] There is no concluding billboard scene in the "OK" script. As discussed below, in the film itself Cosmo just leads the band rather than singing with Kathy and Don.

The penultimate argument establishing a justification for R. F.'s decision to lead the conspiracy to expose Lina's vocal deficiencies was carefully and effectively written up in the first draft back in 1950 by Comden and Green. It appears almost unchanged in the "OK" script as well. The scene is played within one medium shot set in the wings, with one cut to a medium shot of Kathy as she joins the argument. The camera dollies in a little and pans a little, following the dialogue but creating tension in what is, in effect, a slightly varied single two-minute-long take.

The confrontation begins with Cosmo's ironically backhanded compliment to Lina, saying that she "sang as well as Kathy Selden" (1:36:00). Lina tries to persuade R. F. that supporting Kathy's career as an actor, not just a ghost singer, isn't worth jeopardizing the profits he might realize from making Lina's star higher than ever. Ron the publicity man supports her case. Kathy protests that she "just won't do it." Lina points out that Kathy is bound by the five-year contract she signed. Don demands of R. F., "Why don't you tell her [Lina] off?" R. F. does his best with the wooden line, "I don't know, I'm confused. This thing is so big I . . . " before he's mercifully interrupted by Ron urging Don and Lina to take a curtain call.

Lina pushes her luck when she announces that "from now on, I'm running things." R. F. announces that she's "gone a little too far." The crowd demands a speech, Lina insists on making it, and her doom is nigh. At 1:37:53 we see the backs of the three men, their conspiracy sealed, stroll together to watch Lina embarrass herself onstage seconds later. Lina's stage speech is one of Comden and Green's timeless creations. They repeated it from memory in 2002 at a celebration of the release of the 50th Anniversary deluxe two-DVD edition of the film in Los Angeles hosted by Michael Feinstein.[78] Lina finally gets to greet and compliment her fans. But she does so with a tricky triple negative ("ain't / in vain / nothin'"). "If we bring a little joy into your humdrum lives," intones Lina, "our hard work ain't been in vain for nothin.'"[79]

In the "OK" script, Don announces Kathy's identity to the audience. Then Don, singing "You Are My Lucky Star," descends into the audience and leads Kathy back onstage, where they are joined by Cosmo in a trio version of the song as a finale. In the finished film, Don's final speech is shortened. First, as Kathy runs away down the theater's aisle he yells out "Stop her!" We see Kathy trapped, terrified, by a cordon of audience members in the aisle. Don is out of focus, far away onstage. Only then does Don call Kathy "the real star of the picture," yelling out her full name, "Kathy Selden!"

Kathy turns and the camera reverses positions to reveal her tear-streaked face absorbing the news that Don, who had seemingly just betrayed her by making her lip-sync for Lina live, is now giving credit where credit is due, thus betraying Lina.[80] In the "OK" script Don is given the line, "You're going to see an awful lot of us together from now on!" Instead of Comden and Green's final line as written, Don simply repeats, softly, "Kathy," as the camera offers a medium shot of his outstretched arms. Instead of joining the pair in song as in earlier script drafts, as Don sings a cappella in a trembling voice, "You are my lucky star," Cosmo runs to the orchestra conductor and borrows his baton. The elevated camera dollies back and follows him. Following Cosmo's lead, the orchestra sneaks in, supporting Don's still trembling voice.

This reworked version of the film's finale gives Cosmo an active role without horning in on the romantic couple and even makes a virtue of Kelly's expressive but comparatively underpowered singing voice. High satire (Spencer Tracy, a double wedding) has been replaced by nostalgic romance (Kathy's tears, Kelly's a cappella trembling voice). Unfortunately, Kathy must enter the duet by singing the song's four most expressive notes, a relatively high chromatic run back up to the song's starting pitch before the melody again swoops down an octave, equally softly, a vocal embellishment that even her talented vocal double Betty Noyes doesn't pull off convincingly (1:41:37). One of the results of the internet has been remixes by fans of bits of even copyrighted works. At times on YouTube one can find an ingenious remix of the ending, substituting Reynolds's own voice (an outtake from the double CD) for that of Betty Noyes and eliminating the final choral arrangement of "Lucky Star" in favor of an instrumental accompaniment. This gives the avid *Singin'* fan an alternative ending to consider.[81] Kathy's difficult vocal entrance on a rising chromatic scale at the top of the song's range is problematic in both vocal performances—arguably a flaw in the arrangement rather than in either singer's performance.[82]

Freed's lyric at this point, "I was starstruck," is barely plausible, implying an ironic distance from the intense emotions Kathy is supposed to be experiencing at this moment. But in any case, the awkward moment is over quickly. It's the swift pace, abbreviated musical elements, and cinematic storytelling in combination that make this ending effective, albeit entirely without the satire once at the heart of Comden and Green's original ending revealing two newly married celebrity couples and a once-famous actor, now a has-been.

As discussed in chapter 1, both of Comden and Green's ideas are potentially quite funny; they are also powerful sendups of the phenomenon of manufactured, fungible Hollywood celebrity, pioneered during the studio era but with us still. They were abandoned in favor of an unabashedly romantic ending, complete with a heavenly chorus accompanying Kathy and Don as they gaze at each other in front of a billboard advertising their new picture, *Singin' in the Rain* (1:42:11). This striking double image nicely echoes previous plot points involving similar interplays between images and realities: Don's double biography, Lina and Don's contrapuntal love scene during which they embrace passionately while arguing furiously ("I'd rather kiss a tarantula"), and Kathy's doubling of Lina's voice. The camera dollies in for one last close-up before fading out as Don and Kathy clinch.

The remade ending is a fitting climax to Kelly and Donen's many transformations of Comden and Green's pointed sendups of Hollywood, often in favor of dynamic, romantic montages of powerful images accompanied by cut-down dialogue. Some satire was lost, but much was gained, including some of Kelly's most successful, and "most representative," choreography—the subject of the following chapter.[83]

3

Choreography and Cuts

"'Singin' in the Rain' is a summation of Gene Kelly's own work up to
that point, echoing and developing numbers he had done in earlier
films, crystallizing the principles and ideas about dance and film
which he had been forming."

Peter Wollen, *Singin' in the Rain*, 29

Choreography for the Camera

Early in his Broadway career Gene Kelly described his style of choreography as "plenty of pantomime and a good dash of ballet."[1] Film scholar Peter
Wollen has explained how the choreographer's work also functioned within
larger narratives, calling Kelly a creator of "character dance[s] in dramatic
context[s]" who combined vaudeville elements with ballet and "flash"—acrobatics in the Nicholas Brothers mode.[2] While mimetic gestures with the body
are an important part of story ballets, facial expressions generally are not
emphasized. Exploiting the potential of the closeup shot, in his films Kelly
used his face as a mask like a theatrical mime. His stock of facial expressions
included a Buster Keaton-esque stone face (1:27:36), an eyes-sidewise leer
(16:30), a gargoyle's threatening frown (19:02), a resigned ironic grin with
eyes raised to the heavens (1:08:13), and a puzzled, surprised half-smile,
with only half of his upper lip raised (22:44). He also deployed his hands mi-
metically, as frightening claws (15:41), directional paddles (15:42), or bent
back at the wrist, spread wide in supplication (15:45). In *Invitation to the
Dance* (1956) he even appears in full mime makeup and attire: whiteface and
a modified Pierrot costume (5:06). See figures 3.1 and 3.2.

While mime is an important element in his style, Kelly's employment of
ballet vocabulary in *Singin' outside the "Broadway Ballet"* was limited. The
movement in "You Were Meant for Me" is mostly drawn from ballroom
dancing. But the mood of the piece reflects Kelly's adagio approach to ballet,
emphasizing mime and attitudes. His one lift of Reynolds, in "You Were

Singin' in the Rain. Andrew Buchman, Oxford University Press. © Oxford University Press 2024.
DOI: 10.1093/9780197760062.003.0003

Figure 3.1 Kelly's mimetic facial expressions and hand gestures.

Meant for Me," suggests that she was unfamiliar with the ways ballerinas typ-ically use their own muscles and cantilevered weight to make their partner's lifts look more effortless.[3] Compare Reynolds's earnest attempt to support at least some of her own weight on her forearms in figure 3.3 (at 45:28 in the film) with Cyd Charisse's fearless cantilevered perch using Kelly's torso as a fulcrum in the "Broadway Ballet" in figure 3.4 (1:21:28).

All four performers wear hard shoes inappropriate for ballet in these scenes, although Kelly switches to soft-soled shoes and Charisse dances in stocking feet in their second duet in the ballet (1:24:35). Characteristically, Kelly wears pants at all times. He avoids any practical but potentially revealing

Figure 3.2 Kelly as a mime in *Invitation to the Dance* (1956).

Figure 3.3 Kelly lifts Reynolds in "You Were Meant for Me."

Figure 3.4 Kelly lifts Charisse in "Broadway Ballet."

or feminizing costume elements such as the rare leotard-like Harlequin outfit (mostly covered up by a long cloak) he donned for the masked ball in *An American in Paris*.

Kelly and Donen developed an expanded vocabulary for photographing dance, often including the whole figure in the frame (as Fred Astaire consistently did) but from the point of view of a moving camera, adding long shots and close-ups as emphatic punctuation to mark out sections within a number. The co-directors added in many varieties of camera movement— not just crane shots, but pans, tilts, dollies, and changes in point of view, as in "Moses" in *Singin'* when each side of the room serves as a backdrop. Working with MGM's shop staff, Kelly (as previously discussed) also often tinkered with props and costumes, for example employing window drapes as Biblical robes in "Moses" and couches as teetertotters in "Good Morning."

Kelly had already employed elaborate special effects such as a composited cartoon mouse or a doppelgänger as dance partners in earlier films, but there are only a few overt special effects in *Singin'* aside from Donen's magnum opus, the montages set to the "Beautiful Girl" medley.[4] The film's opening shot of the trio version of "Singin' in the Rain" involves a subtle composite shot. The dancers march briskly in rhythm toward the camera but remain exactly the same size, presumably because they're striding along treadmills obscured by a grey fog at the bottom of the frame (0:00:29). A rain effect is also superimposed on the image. The credit sequence was originally shot without umbrellas, then reshot late in production, perhaps after the multiple treadmills used in the "Broadway Ballet" were set up.[5] In an analogous special effect, compositing two shots together creates the impression of impossibly long crane shots at the beginning and end of the "Broadway Ballet" (1:16:19 and 1:28:29).

As Wollen observed, as a choreographer Kelly often focused on "character dance[s]," de-emphasizing large ensembles and chorus lines in favor of personality-driven solos, duets, and trios showcasing the strengths of particular performers.[6] Small ensembles predominate in *Singin'*, but the size and tempi are carefully varied. See table 3.1.

Table 3.1 Dance Numbers in Chronological Order

Described by Ensemble Type, Tempo, and Soloists
Dancers without fictional names are listed by [performer's name]

1	TRIO	"Singing in the Rain"	FAST	Kathy, Don, Cosmo
2	DUET	"Fit as a Fiddle"	FAST	Don, Cosmo
3	ENSEMBLE	"All I Do Is Dream of You"	FAST	Kathy
4	SOLO	"Make 'Em Laugh"	FAST	Cosmo
5	ENSEMBLE	"Beautiful Girl" Medley	MODERATE	[Jimmy Thompson]*
6	DUET	"You Were Meant for Me"	SLOW	Kathy, Don
7	DUET	"Moses Supposes"	FAST	Don, Cosmo, [Bobby Watson]
8	TRIO	"Good Morning"	FAST	Kathy, Don, Cosmo
9	SOLO	"Singing in the Rain" (reprise)	SLOW	Don
10	ENSEMBLE	"Broadway Ballet"	VARIOUS	Don, [Cyd Charisse]**
11	DUET	"You Are My Lucky Star"	SLOW	Kathy, Don

N.B.: Numbers with minimal movement are omitted; these are "Would You?" (twice) and "Singin' in the Rain" (second reprise; although Lina flaps her arms and the men all imitate her).

*Uncredited in *Singin'*, Thompson danced in Comden and Green's first Freed assignment *Good News* (1947) and was Frank Sinatra's stand-in on *Take Me Out to the Ball Game* (1947). He also appeared in *Brigadoon* (1954).

**Charisse's character has no spoken dialogue and no name.

The two middle duets are as different as they could be: an adagio pas de deux for Reynolds and Kelly ("You Were Meant for Me") and (after "Fit as a Fiddle") a second up-tempo male duet for O'Connor and Kelly, "Moses." This second duet is arguably a trio. Don's adroitly hapless diction coach (Bobby Watson) is pushed around mercilessly by both male dancers, becoming a live version of the dummy O'Connor employs as a quasi-partner in "Make 'Em Laugh" and the raincoat he dances with, then kicks out of the frame in "Good Morning."[7]

Each of the three ensemble dances in the film is larger than the last, culminating in the ballet. The first, "All I Do Is Dream of You," is fully diegetic, integrated into the story as an entertainment at R. F.'s post-premiere party. In the second ensemble, set to a medley of songs anchored by "Beautiful Girl," the choreography serves the camera, providing a repetitive motion or pattern for each tricky shot.[8] Donen packed in plenty of unusual special effects using compositing, off-axis tilts of the camera body, and slow, fast, and reverse motion. Simply comparing this number to Busby Berkeley's work is a disservice to Donen. He goes the master one better, creating his own visions of Berkeley's characteristic Petipa-and-beyond patterns. Both Kelly and Donen had worked with Berkeley, who had directed *Take Me Out to the Ball Game*. The older director afforded them opportunities to co-direct scenes and sequences for that film.[9]

The first minute of the "Beautiful Girl" medley contains twenty-three separate shots, including many involving special effects, sometimes connected with elaborate vintage-style wipes that sweep across the screen from multiple directions at once (34:34). The sequence begins with two swirling issues of *Variety*, then another that magically moves backward in time, unburning itself. In many of the shots, sparkling backdrops in a variety of pastel colors twinkle. In one such scene a trio of Slavic male dancers romp against such a backdrop in midair, with no floor below them. A quartet of male singers seems to be flat on their backs on the floor singing, and a pinwheel of dancers emerges out of a singer's megaphone in shots made from above. These shots aren't imitations; they are Donen's inventions in the style of Berkeley.

Two more moments emblematic of Donen's witty eye are analogous shots of dancers' legs. A psychedelic line of disembodied dancers' legs assembled via masking and compositing is cleverly complemented by a similar shot achieved quite simply by comparison, in a downward-pointing live shot of a chorus line's disembodied tapping feet and legs (34:58 and 35:07). Yet another tribute to Berkeley's kaleidoscopic choreography constitutes the climax of the number.[10] In this shot from above, the lilac-grey chorus line and the models from the fashion show in their various multicolored outfits assemble in concentric circles around the singer. Orange-red, magenta, and yellow costume elements are carefully spaced around the outside of the human flower thus produced. The outer circle of dancers echoes the singer's outstretched arms while joining hands. Kathy, almost unrecognizable, is nevertheless placed as prominently as possible given the composition, at bottom center in the circle of grey dancers (38:39). See figure 3.5.

Figure 3.5 Disembodied legs in composite and tilt shots and the final overhead shot in "Beautiful Girl."

New pages inserted into the "OK" screenplay dated May 23 describe the complex montages and the performance of "Beautiful Girl" but not the fashion show, suggesting that it was interpolated into the scene later.[11] Fordin described this as a decision initiated by Donen and costumer designer Walter Plunkett.[12] Also according to Fordin, Edens wrote the spoken narration for the new sequence describing twelve outfits, one for each month of the year.[13] Dabholkar and Hess downrate the fashion show, calling it "the only unnecessary section in the entire movie."[14] It may be, but the entire show of tableaux vivants is less than ninety seconds long, and the outfits are out of this world. Observing the involuntary, slight movements of the live models as they pose, one is reminded of Kelly's many mimetic moments of stillness throughout the film, only sampled in the collection assembled into figure 3.1. The magazine-style show also calls to mind the fabulous shot of two gum-chewing fans clutching a fan magazine, *Screen Digest*, with LOCKWOOD & LAMONT" on the cover dressed in matching white turtlenecks and tan plaids during the movie's quasi-documentary coverage of the premiere of *The Royal Rascal* (1:59). Taken altogether, the "Beautiful Girl" sequence combines journalistic and cinematic responses to the challenges of making talkies. The disembodied legs in figure 3.5 and a short wedding gown with a long train and an immense veil piled up behind the model in the fashion show (38:00) prefigure elements that also appear in Kelly's "Broadway Ballet," discussed below. The whole fantastic sequence switches back to diegesis smoothly when it turns out that "Beautiful Girl" is just one scene in Zelda's new talking, singing, dancing picture (35:53).

Only Kelly sings in the next number, Don and Kathy's subsequent slow pas de deux to "You Were Meant for Me." The dance is set in a faux sunset Don conjures up on an empty soundstage, another great self-reflexive depiction of movie magic in the making, underscored with musical commentaries like a flute uttering bird calls as Kelly announces "colored lights in a garden" (41:59). Kathy's dress (just like those worn by the other ten dancers in "Beautiful Girl") incorporates translucent veil-like material that flutters in the breeze from a gently turning wind machine; fans also provide off-camera supercharging to the "Broadway Ballet" sequence in which Cyd Charisse and Kelly dance with a gigantic ribbon of gauzy fabric.

A quick zoom in on a fourth newspaper front page headline harking back to the "Beautiful Girl" montage, underscored with a brass fanfare followed by a string tremolo overlaid with frantically rapid brass riffs, leads efficiently into the following thoroughly comic diction coach scenes and "Moses" (46:12 and 48:14). Again, the directors develop both these scenes considerably beyond their origins, quick ideas added to the "temporary complete" first draft screenplay between September and October 1950. As mentioned, Donen's virtuoso camerawork uses two sides of the "room" as background. During the presto section in Lloyd "Skip" Martin's propulsive swing band arrangement for "Moses" the camera frames the two dancers so tightly that it seems to be hand-held at times, making repeated minute adjustments in tilt and pan (50:22).

"Good Morning" employs a range of costumes and props in an indoor dance; Robert Alton created an analogous energetic duet for O'Connor and Reynolds, "Where Did You Learn to Dance?", in an even smaller living room set the following year in *I Love Melvin* (1953). Kelly's famous solo version of the title song receives special attention in chapter 4, where we'll also revisit "Make 'Em Laugh" and "Good Morning," focusing in on the starting point for Kelly's choreography and Donen's cinematography, the music.

The "Broadway Ballet" (aka "Broadway Melody")

Despite its length and lavish production, the ballet is perhaps the most neglected portion of *Singin' in the Rain*. This is reflected even in its variable title, either the "Broadway Ballet" or "Broadway Melody," the song upon which the score is based, along with another old Brown and Freed song, "Broadway Rhythm." Rehearsals for the ballet began on August 20.[15] Kelly recorded his audio tracks on October 12 and 13. The finale with seventy dancers was shot in a space the size of two American football fields created by joining up two large soundstages.[16] With Kelly dividing his time between various unfinished details and work on prospective new projects, shooting continued until the week before Thanksgiving, wrapping on November 21. According to Dabholkar and Hess, the ballet cost exactly $605,960 to shoot—roughly $7 million in 2024 dollars, more than the ballet in *An American in Paris* cost.[17] See table 3.2 for a breakdown of sections within the piece.[18]

Only two sections, Charisse and Kelly's two duets, last two minutes or more. Six sections in boldface in the table are more central to the narrative of this story ballet, the tale of a dancer's rise to fame, romantic disappointment, and return to dancing. The rhythmic flips of silver coins, first by the hoods, then (in a gender-bending surprise) by Charisse, constitute a visual

Table 3.2 Sections in the "Broadway Ballet"

#	Short Description	Size	Modes	Starts at	Length
1	Don: "Broadway Rhythm"	Solo	Song	1:15:33	0:00:43
2	Ensemble enters (transition)	Ensemble	Dance	1:16:16	0:00:14
3	Don moves through the city	Ensemble	Dance	1:16:30	0:00:36
4	**Don auditions for agents**	Duets	Song & Dance	1:17:06	0:00:34
5	Agent changes Don's costume	Duet	Dance	1:17:40	0:00:13
6	Audience greets Don	Ensemble also sings	Song & Dance	1:17:53	0:00:16
7	**Don performs "Broadway Rhythm"**	Ensemble	Song & Dance	1:18:09	0:01:03
8	Don	Solo	Tap Dance	1:19:12	0:00:34
9	**Cyd, Don, three hoods meet**	Duet	Dance	1:19:46	0:02:26
10	Head hood proffers diamonds	Small Ensemble	Mime	1:22:12	0:00:26
11	Agent changes Don's venues	Ensemble	Mime	1:22:38	0:00:10
12	Columbia Burlesque: Don as Clown	Ensemble	Song & Dance	1:22:48	0:00:16
13	Palace Vaudeville: Don as Yankee	Ensemble	Song & Dance	1:23:04	0:00:16
14	**Ziegfeld Follies: Don as Swell**	Ensemble	Song & Dance	1:23:20	0:00:17
15	Applause, roulette wheel	None	Montage	1:23:37	0:00:07
16	Casino Waltz	Ensemble	Dance	1:23:44	0:00:23
17	Don spies Cyd		Zoom shots	1:24:07	0:00:12
18	Cyd stands in wedding dress	Wind machine	Mime (with wind machine)	1:24:19	0:00:15
19	**Don's Dream: Veil Duet with Cyd**	Duet	Dance (with wind machine)	1:24:34	0:02:00
20	Lap dissolve back to casino			1:26:34	0:00:04
21	Cyd shuns Don, joins hood		Mime	1:26:38	0:00:33
22	Don leaves club, dejected	Solo	Mime	1:27:11	0:00:27
23	New dancer comes to town		Song & Dance	1:27:38	0:00:13
24	**Don rejoins the fray**		**Song & Dance**	**1:27:51**	**0:00:10**
25	Ensemble re-enters		Dance	1:28:01	0:00:28
26	Don: "Broadway Melody"		Song & Composited Shots	1:28:29	0:00:19
27	Lap dissolve back to screening room			1:28:48	
	TOTAL LENGTH				0:13:15

motif connecting several different sections. Charisse wears a Louise Brooks–style wig created by Sydney Guillaroff in most of the ballet, but a variety of costumes.[19]

The first duet is set in an improbably gigantic speakeasy in which Kelly achieves his first success as a performer. A variety of extras had to remain frozen in position to create tableaux vivants in the background; at least they were seated at cocktail tables, making it easier to hold their positions through multiple takes. In one of the most memorable scenes in the film, Kelly slides into the camera with an exaggerated clown face denoting astonishment, confronting Charisse's extended foot en pointe, on which his discarded felt porkpie hat is perched (1:19:46). Following Kelly's roving eyes, the camera crawls along Charisse's horizontal leg, then slowly up her torso to her face.[20] As still as a statue, she releases puffs of cigarette smoke, first from her nose, then from her mouth, recalling a famous smoking billboard long situated in New York's Times Square theater district (1:19:56). This voyeuristic tracking shot is accompanied by a steamy low clarinet solo (eventually joined by a chorus of saxophones), punctuated by stabs from percussion and brass in Conrad Salinger's ambitious score. Charisse chooses to leave the three hoods she's sitting with. The head gangster, played by Carl Milletaire, is memorably made up with a lurid artificial scar high on one cheek, an exaggerated homage to Paul Muni's makeup in *Scarface* (1932).

Charisse dances around Kelly, who keeps looking, then looking away, taking a dip at one point reminiscent of his recent impersonation of the clown Rafael Padilla (known as Chocolat) in the ballet in *An American in Paris*[21] (1:20:53). Although Kelly becomes more active after Charisse thrusts her cigarette holder into his mouth and he angrily throws it away, he continues to partner supportively, lifting and steadying Charisse as she spins and dips to the floor, using Kelly as a fulcrum. Kelly's naive attempt to kiss Charisse can't compete with a glittering diamond bracelet proffered by the gangster she came in with (1:22:16).

In her second duet with Kelly, enacting Kelly's fantasy on seeing her again across a crowded room, Charisse doffs the cloche-style wig and lets her hair down (held in place by a sparkling double band resembling a tiara). She wears a modified wedding gown with a flying gossamer train many yards long, on an abstract modernist set made up of long steps in front of a vast cyclorama lit in shades of pink, purple, and grey. The set was perhaps inspired by other dream sequences including Salvador Dalí's famous designs for the black-and-white dream sequence in Alfred Hitchcock's *Spellbound* (1945).

Some of Joseph Urban's scenic designs for the Metropolitan Opera and the *Ziegfeld Follies* in the 1920s were similarly abstract.[22]

Again Charisse is the prima ballerina; Kelly supports and lifts her, often kneeling below her as she dances. The couple kiss, to a musical climax marked by a loud cymbal crash (1:26:13). After a dissolve back to the crowded night-club, Charisse coldly repels Kelly's importuning, revealing her alliance with the head mobster by flipping a coin expertly herself, then tossing it to Kelly in a gesture of dismissal before rejoining her companion (1:26:51).

The ballet's detachment from the rest of the story in *Singin'* can make it seem to be a dispensable part of the film. Like "Make 'Em Laugh," the ballet is functionally but superficially integrated into the film via perfunctory framing dialogue. The prologue and postlude in a screening room giving the ballet a narrative frame were the last shots to be filmed, on December 26, 1951.[23] Because of its length and intermittent gravitas, unlike the equally diverting "Make 'Em Laugh" the ballet may never escape the stigma of being an unnecessary if elegant appendage. However, there are plenty of visual connections to the rest of the film.

References to the 1920s abound. Kelly enters in a flat hat and glasses reminiscent of the silent film comedian Harold Lloyd's typical attire. In their first duet Cyd disposes of his hat and his glasses before (as previously mentioned) gently placing her long cigarette holder into Kelly's mouth. Later in the ballet, Kelly's subsequent progress through four progressively more upscale venues as a performer (speakeasy, burlesque house, vaudeville house, and Broadway theater) recapitulates analogous steps in Don's visual biography in the first minutes of the film (pool hall, restaurant, vaudeville houses, and silent films).

While there are few direct connections between *Singin'* and the many previous MGM films featuring songs by Freed and Brown, *Broadway Melody of 1936* also contains an elaborate penultimate production number in five parts based on the song "Broadway Rhythm," which made its debut in that picture. The huge number is followed by a very brief finale depicting the ingénue couple's engagement. To the tune of "You Are My Lucky Star," Robert Taylor sings, "You are my Shearer, Crawford, Hepburn, Harlow, and my Garbo" to Eleanor Powell by way of proposal. In a 1958 interview Roger Edens fondly remembered devising this scheme. "It was like a little revue, and audiences went wild over it."[24] Perhaps Kelly's "Broadway Ballet" should also be considered as a deliberately episodic revue or suite, not a Rodgers and Hammerstein–style integrated dream ballet.

Donen later said that "the 'Broadway Melody–Broadway Rhythm' ballet was an interruption to the main thrust of *Singin' in the Rain*."[25] Stuart Hall and Paddy Whannel also felt that *Singin'* was "flawed by a rather pretentious ballet sequence."[26] Kara Gardner has discussed the lack of narrative integration between the "Broadway Melody" (her preferred title) and the film as a whole, and points out that it is not a dream ballet depicting a main character's fantasy like Laurey's dream ballet in *Oklahoma!* (1943 onstage, 1955 on film). Instead Kelly created a "fantasy dance sequence."[27] Ideally, she writes, a dream ballet "explore[s] a main character in some depth. But the piece ["Broadway Melody"] serves as a digression. It tells the story of an unnamed hoofer, not Don Lockwood."

Nevertheless, if the "Beautiful Girl" montage is a hyperactive parody of massive musical extravaganzas (including dream ballets), then the "Broadway Ballet" itself offers a more generous form of engagement and revision. Although Gardner correctly points out that the sequence does not explicitly explore the "subconscious feelings and motivations of a main character," perhaps one can read the ballet as a dual exploration of the repressed sexuality of Don's character, who reforms from a Lothario with roving hands into a model suitor after Kathy re-enters his life, and of Kelly's own repressed sexuality. Gene Kelly's daughter Kerry recalled that in the late 1940s it seemed that "most intellectuals and most creative people were in psychoanalysis. . . . The only person I knew growing up who was not in psychoanalysis was my father."[28] The male dancer in the ballet can be interpreted not just as another side of Kelly as Don Lockwood but as a fictionalized projection of Kelly himself.

In Adolph Green's words, Charisse "comes out of nowhere and has nothing to do with the story," but "she was so terrific we really thought she was going to engulf the whole thing. It was suddenly about her. She was just great."[29] However, there are visual cues connecting the ballet to earlier dance numbers featuring Reynolds. Charisse wears a stunningly short green cocktail "dress," more like a leotard, similar in outline to Reynolds's pastel pink skirted bathing costume in "All I Do Is Think of You."

Charisse next appears in a jaw-dropping wedding dress with the veil worn as a train, with sequins arranged like festoons of icing on a wedding cake, recalling both the moment when Reynolds pops out of a giant cake and the moment when she throws a cake at Don and hits Lina instead. Finally, Charisse dances in a stylized version of the wedding dress with a famously long veil moved around by wind machines. Recall that Reynolds wore a lilac-grey day dress covered from neck to knee in a chiffon veil in the love duet "You Were Meant for Me," and a wind machine was an integral part of the staging of that number as well.

Dabholkar and Hess interpret Charisse's character as a "vamp," a gangster's moll toying with Kelly, who presents himself as a captivated innocent rather than as an equal in experience.[30] Hats, cigarettes, eyeglasses, female legs, a shockingly short wedding dress and incredibly long veil can all be interpreted readily as quasi-Freudian props. Charisse's costumes are licentious, and her screen presence is electric. At some moments she is depicted as the aggressor, as when she takes off Kelly's spectacles. At other points, Kelly abases himself before parts of her body, most famously when he slides across the floor on his knee and arrives, kneeling, at the base of Charisse's extended leg at the beginning of their first duet. Predictably, moments like these led to the film's one serious brush with Hollywood's studio-sponsored central censorship office.

After screening the film in December the censors attached one zinger to the certificate of approval they transmitted to new studio head Dore Schary on January 3, 1952: a demand that "in all prints to be released of this picture, the first dance sequence involving Gene Kelly and Cyd Charisse will be shortened on the basis of the elimination discussed by Mr. Vogel of M.G.M. and Mr. Van Schmus of this office on December 28, 1951."[31] This ultimatum may explain the very brief jump cut within an otherwise continuous medium long shot (1:22:02). The sensuality of Charisse's character also led to a "B" rating from the Legion of Decency, one of the faith-based organizations whose protests in the 1930s had led to the hegemony of Breen's office. Some state censors objected, but evidently further cuts to the ballet were only necessary for a few foreign markets: Indonesia, Pakistan, and Francoist Spain.[32]

Previews (or Cost Considerations) Lead to Cuts

In two previews, the film received many positive ratings. The first preview took place at the De Anza Theatre in Riverside, California, on December 21, 1951. The film received overall ratings from 193 participating respondents in the audience. Ninety rated the film as "Outstanding," fifty-seven "Excellent," thirty-seven "Very Good," two "Good," and one "Fair."[33] The second preview, at the Bay Theatre in Pacific Palisades, California, on December 27, 1951, garnered 250 rating cards from the audience, 108 of whom chose

"Outstanding," ninety-two "Excellent," thirty-four "Very Good," eleven "Good," and four "Fair."[34]

Despite these positive results, Freed (in consultation with the co-directors and fellow executives) prescribed about twenty minutes' worth of surgical nips and tucks in early 1952, detailed in a memorandum.[35] See table 3.3 for a synopsis.

The cuts included solo versions of two numbers already included elsewhere in the film, "You Are My Lucky Star" and "All I Do Is Dream of You." Debbie Reynolds's solo performance of "You Are My Lucky Star" sung to an image of Kelly on a billboard on the studio lot was cut. A slow solo song and dance version of "All I Do Is Dream of You" performed by Kelly in his bedroom after Kathy's up-tempo performance of the same song, firmly establishing his fascination with her in an appropriate setting for a song about dreams, was also cut. A two-minute-long pool party scene set at Don's

Table 3.3 Post-Production Cuts to *Singin' in the Rain*

Scene(s)	Setting(s)	Timing (seconds)	Sunk Costs
Scene 15.1	Street Corner Fruit Stand	0:17	$4,013
Scenes 31.1–4	Billboards	0:13	$3,322
Scene 31.6	Exterior of Don's House	1:59	$4,889
Scenes 31.8 & 46	Interior of Chinese Theatre	0:58	$5,680
Scenes 51-56	Interior of the Simpson Mansion	1:26	$10,550
Scenes 57x1-2	**Exterior and Interior of Don's House** ("All I Do Is Dream of You")	**3:57**	**$61,244**
Scenes 60A & 60.1	Stage	1:37	$5,335
Scenes 70x1-2	Musical Montage	1:06	$10,210
Scene 70x3	Stage for "Beautiful Girl" Number	1:57	$7,790
Scene 76x1	**Billboard ("You Are My Lucky Star")**	**4:03**	**$21,972**
Scenes 88-109	Exterior and Interior of Theatre	0:45	$4,515
(no scene indicated)	Sound Stage	0:45	$3,465
TOTALS		19:03	$142,985

Source: Los Angeles, Academy Library, Rudy Behlmer Papers, Folder 47: "America's Favorite Movies—research (SINGIN' IN THE RAIN). In this folder are filed sixteen large notecards filled with notes made at USC and Academy Libraries ("ACADEMY"), one notecard-size photocopy of a newspaper article, and a copy of the document of cuts, below, with underlines added in pencil (by Behlmer, for emphasis?). There is also a copy of this document at USC, in the Arthur Freed Papers, Box 23, Folder 1, titled "eliminations made from Singing in the rain [*sic*]," with a cover memo from J. J. Cohn to Freed and Donen dated April 11, 1952.

house was cut from his autobiography early in the film (scene 31.6), along with banter between Cosmo and women at R. F.'s premiere party (scenes 51–56). The dialogue written around Don's reunion with Kathy after the "Beautiful Girl" medley (scene 70x3) was trimmed extensively, including lines for Zelda Zanders (played by Rita Moreno) urging R. F. not to offer Kathy a bigger part in the film.[36] As mentioned in the preface, the double DVD release of *Singin' in the Rain* overseen by film historian Rudy Behlmer includes audio recordings, some film footage, and still photographs of the sets for these cut scenes.[37]

Both the solos elaborate on points made effectively elsewhere in the film.[38] Leaving Don alone on the steps of R. F.'s mansion after failing to catch up with Kathy lets the lover's duet "You Were Meant for Me" stand alone as his confession of romantic interest. If Kathy's characterization is shortchanged by leaving out her solo version of "Lucky Star," nevertheless the number didn't move the story forward. One significant thematic loss is visual. The absence of the focus on a giant billboard featuring Don and Lina facing one another removes an ironic sting from the movie's final billboard scene, where Lina is simply replaced by the younger Kathy, who (in true patriarchal Hollywood fashion) might simply be replaced in turn in a few more years by yet another ingénue partnering Don onscreen as the sexist Hollywood star machinery ground on. But removing Kathy's billboard solo strengthens the film as a romance by omitting a visual reminder of the evanescence of Hollywood love affairs in general.

Somehow word went around Hollywood concerning the fairly drastic series of cuts. In his "Rambling Reporter" column, Mike Connolly of the *Hollywood Reporter* commented on March 14, 1952, exaggerating somewhat, "Add two numbers and MGM has another musical in what it cut from 'Singin' in the Rain.'"[39] Dabholkar and Hess attribute the decision to cut the two solos to comments from preview audiences.[40] This seems doubtful, since both Kelly and Reynolds received overwhelmingly high ratings overall. It seems more likely that Freed, Donen, and Kelly came up with an effective set of cuts that stripped the narrative of any extraneous material while increasing the number of possible screenings of the film per day per theater. The studio's confidence in the film as cut was strong; on the previous day the *Hollywood Reporter* announced that MGM had ordered 500 release prints of *Singin'*, "one of the largest domestic and foreign print orders ever placed by the company for a Technicolor film."[41] Cutting out one sixth of the film's length reduced duplication and distribution costs as well.

Billboard Dreams: Kathy's Cut Solo Song

After reuniting with Don on the Monumental Pictures lot where she's been hired for a part as Zelda Zanders's kid sister (a role type Reynolds previously played in *The Daughter of Rosie O'Grady* and *Two Weeks with Love*), Kathy sings "You Are My Lucky Star" while gazing at an image of Don on a billboard. She sings for herself, rather than being dubbed. The scene makes theatrical sense of Freed's lyrics comparing romance with a movie star to opening "heaven's portal here on earth" by having Kathy romance not a person but an image. She is contemplating her feelings for someone who tried to seduce her on their first meeting, then mocked her artistic aspirations at a second meeting that ended disastrously when Lina's face caught the cake.

Finally, at their third in-person encounter, Don has become a supportive colleague and perhaps more than that. If, in addition, Reynolds had been allowed to sing in her own youthful gutsy way, the result might have been another hit record to follow up her rendition of "Aba Daba Honeymoon" in 1950. Kelly's assistants Jeanne Coyne and Carol Haney gave Reynolds the support she needed to dance with Kelly and O'Connor. But perhaps time didn't permit the same attention to showcasing her potential strengths as a vocalist such as the engaging contrast between her chest and head vocal ranges, and addressing her weaknesses, such as an occasional inaccurate pitch in an era when audio technology couldn't ameliorate this fault. The number powerfully illustrated Comden and Green's explorations of the power of images and stars, still a major theme in the finished film. Roger Edens's added verse and monologue describing Don's multicolored outfit on a previous outing to the celebrity restaurant The Brown Derby is also hilariously, queerly, over the top.[42]

Bedroom Dreams: Don's Cut Solo Song and Dance

Kelly's solo version of "All I Do Is Dream of You" was the last number to be shot, completed on November 21, 1951. Although the footage is lost, an audio recording and black and white still photographs of the set survive.[43] Despite the leisurely pace of most of the underscoring, Donen later described Kelly's dancing in the cut scene as "very athletic."[44] According to biographer Clive Hirschhorn, Kelly regarded the dance "as one of the best he has ever done."[45] Possibly, Hirschhorn was relying not on direct testimony from Kelly but from the usually reliable Rudy Behlmer's 1982 account of the cut scenes. Behlmer wrote, "Kelly regarded it as one of his best," comparing it to another slow ballad cut from *An American in Paris,* "I've Got a Crush on You."[46] The Assistant Director's Report for this final day of production revealed smooth progress and a wrap at 2:37 p.m., giving the cast and crew a little extra time to prepare for the Thanksgiving holiday the next day.

The audio track was recorded on April 4, indicating that it was a firm addition to the production before shooting began.[47] But the new number was barely sketched out by Comden and Green in the "OK" script dated April 11, suggesting that Kelly and Donen were comfortable fleshing out the details in rehearsals during the production period. The writers envisioned Kelly breaking into the song in the driveway after Kathy drives away, then a dissolve to Kelly in his bedroom continuing to sing in his pajamas. The beginning of both the scene and its new arrangement did make it into the final cut (25:02–25:36). A fan-made online amalgam has segued the end of the party scene ending on a freeze frame superimposed with the subtitle "Footage Lost" to the preserved audio track for the lost scene (at 1:23).[48] The musical arrangement for this scene is credited to Conrad Salinger, blessed with an exceptional, lush, romantic musical imagination; Salinger's short score was then transcribed into a full score and parts for a chamber orchestra by Bob Franklyn.[49] MGM's original musical arrangements were themselves a fungible commodity, published as sheet music in 1952 after the film opened.[50]

The narrative setup for the scene is primarily pantomimed by Kelly much as in the setup for the solo version of "Singing in the Rain." Kathy's stand-in drives her car away as Don opens the front door of R. F.'s mansion in a long shot (25.01). Don runs toward the camera, calling out, "Kathy!" twice. The camera moves closer, and Don runs directly toward it (25:06). This kind of motion toward the camera was one of Kelly's preferred ways of enhancing the immediacy of dance numbers on film by breaking the picture plane; here we see it used more conventionally to dramatize a character's forward motion. Don yells, "Hey!" and a plaintive cello enters, playing a solo line that winds slowly upward (supported by more strings), a musical representation of Don's loneliness and disappointment.[51]

Don turns to go back into the party (25.13), then waves impatiently and turns again toward the camera, staring into the distance after Kathy. He puts his hands in his pockets, getting hold of himself. The cello winds back down (25.20). Don pushes his tongue into the corner of his mouth, then smiles ruefully. The scene dissolves to the gate of Monumental Pictures, daytime (i.e., time has passed). The cello bridges the gap, and an English horn sounds a low, chant-like call that is overlaid on the soundtrack with the sputter from the exhaust of a black sedan taxiing through the studio gate (25:31).

The cello and English horn solos are all that remain in the film of the lush orchestral arrangement of "All I Do Is Dream of You" co-credited to Lennie Hayton and Salinger.[52] If the number had been retained, it would have been the longest in the film except for the ballet, at four and half minutes. Fortunately, the music itself was recorded and preserved; it deserves a second hearing. One can only hope that the lost film footage will resurface some day.

Brevity Is the Soul of Wit—and Integration?

It was not unusual for studio films to undergo cuts in post-production. After all, it's much more complicated to reassemble a given cast and set if additional takes are needed. Better by far to overshoot and then throw away some footage that turns out to be redundant or otherwise extraneous. What is more unusual is for cuts to result in a markedly improved film. Both the coherence and the concision of *Singin'* appear to have been enhanced by Donen and his co-workers in the editing suite, sparking comments like Comden and Green's quoted at the outset of this book, "There isn't a wasted second."[53] If Comden and Green's screenplay became less satirical as a result, the comedy remained, perhaps strengthened by simpler dialogue and more concise editing. "Comedy," Comden once averred, defending their reputation against a charge of being light and fizzy compared to later Broadway creators like Stephen Sondheim and Michael Bennett, "is very hard to do."[54] The alternately lush and lively musical arrangements prepared for Kelly to work with stand up very well over time for the most part. See table 3.4.

Table 3.4 lays out the final length of each number, the portions of the film that Comden and Green specifically acknowledged Kelly and Donen created. Musical numbers take up about 40 percent of the film's final cut—another fact bolstering Donen's claims of greater authorship discussed earlier. Although numbers now predominate, two major intervals without dance or song also stand out in this table: fifteen minutes after the first energetic male duet "Fit as a Fiddle" and ten minutes after the second, "Moses." These nonmusical intervals strengthen Basinger's description of *Singin'* as a history, comedy, and romance as well as a musical. Note that only two of Kathy's numbers were dubbed by Betty Noyes—but these are placed prominently toward the

Table 3.4 Finalized Order and Duration of Musical Numbers
(dance numbers in boldface; intervals in grey italic boldface)

	Title	Starts at	Ends at	Duration
1	"Singin' in the Rain" (Kathy, Cosmo, Don)	0:00:21	0:01:38	0:01:17
—	Boy (young Don) tap dancing in pool room	0:04:56	0:05:10	0:00:14
—	Bar quartet (Don, violin; Cosmo, piano)	0:05:26	0:05:34	0:00:08
—	Clowns (Cosmo, Don)	0:05:35	0:05:47	0:00:12
2	"Fit as a Fiddle" (Cosmo, Don)	0:05:48	0:07:28	0:01:40
	Interval [dialogue, action, underscoring] (15:20)	*0:07:28*	*0:22:48*	
3	"All I Do Is Dream of You" (Kathy [inaudible], ensemble)	0:22:48	0:24:12	0:01:24
4	"Make 'Em Laugh" (Cosmo)	0:27:12	0:30:50	0:03:38
5a	"Beautiful Girl Montage" (Jimmy Thompson, ensemble)	0:34:42	0:36:46	0:02:04
	"I've Got a Feelin' You're Foolin'," "The Wedding of the Painted Doll," "Should I?" and "Beautiful Girl"			
6	Fashion Show (spoken and sung with underscoring)	0:36:46	0:38:12	0:01:26
5b	"Beautiful Girl" (Jimmy Thompson, ensemble)	0:38:12	0:38:44	0:00:32
7	"You Were Meant for Me" (Don)	0:42:40	0:46:12	0:03:32
8	"Moses" (Cosmo, Don)	0:48:38	0:51:20	0:02:42
	Interval [dialogue, action, underscoring] (10:28)	*0:51:20*	*1:01:48*	
9	"Good Morning" (Kathy, Cosmo, Don)	1:01:48	1:05:02	0:03:14
10	"Singin' in the Rain" (reprise) (Don)	1:07:54	1:11:52	0:03:58
11a	"Would You?" (Kathy [dubbed by Betty Noyes])	1:13:30	1:15:10	0:01:40
12	"Broadway Ballet" (Don, ensemble, underscoring)			
	"The Broadway Melody" and "Broadway Rhythm"	1:15:33	1:28:46	0:13:13
11b	"Would You?" (reprise) (Kathy [dubbed by Betty Noyes])	1:34:32	1:35:40	0:01:08
13	"Singin' in the Rain" (second reprise) (Kathy)	1:39:32	1:40:48	0:01:16
14	"You Are My Lucky Star" (Kathy [dubbed by Betty Noyes], Don)	1:41:07	1:42:44	0:01:37
	Subtotal			44:55

end of the film. In any case, we actually hear Reynolds singing only three times: in the opening and closing performances of "Singing in the Rain," and in "Good Morning." Her voice is inaudible in "All I Do Is Dream of You" and, like Charisse in the ballet, she dances mutely in both "You Were Meant for Me" and "Beautiful Girl."

Aside from the ballet, the four longest numbers in the film are all less than four minutes long: Kelly's solo "Singing in the Rain," O'Connor's solo "Make 'Em Laugh," Reynolds and Kelly's duet "You Were Meant for Me," and the trio "Good Morning." O'Connor and Kelly's second duet, "Moses," is also close to three minutes in length. It is certainly true that each of these numbers is framed by introductory action and dialogue that lead into the scene and sometimes closely related material just following the dance leading the audience back out to the ongoing narrative. This connecting material is one major mode of integration, and although it is often perfunctory, it is also often effective.[55]

The actors' eloquent gestures and faces in dialogue and action scenes constitute another source of quasi-choreographic integration, blurring the lines between dance and drama. One is likely to remember Kelly driving a motorcycle off a cliff, sneaking into a wooden shed that then explodes, atop a streetcar, or smiling, as well as Kelly dancing and singing (9:22, 9:32, 15:30, and 1:08:54). Hagen often seemed to bring out the best intemperate expressions in the men around her, and of course, her vocal timbres can be exquisitely painful (13:13).

Singin' has no dance finale, just a compressed musical finale less than two minutes long ("You Are My Lucky Star"). Another justification for the "Broadway Ballet" is that it acts as an anticipatory fulfillment of expectations for an ambitious musical number at a musical film's end. Placing the ballet earlier in the narrative clears the way for a more streamlined, tightly cut finale that might otherwise disappoint some in the audience.[56]

Kelly's choreography for *Singin'* is highly competent but derived in part from strategies developed in earlier movies and other numbers like the trio "Make Way for Tomorrow." The "Alter Ego" dance in *Cover Girl* (1944) and the construction site dance in *Living in a Big Way* (1947, with music by Hayton) both early collaborations with Donen, are pieces in which Kelly performs solos that combine cinematic bricolage, joyful athleticism, and a skilled mime's able acting with virtuosity and emotional intensity. In these previous experiments Kelly and Donen explored just how far special effects and dynamic camerawork could go to deepen the two-dimensional frame and still serve the dancer and the dance.

In contrast, what distinguishes the numbers in *Singin'* is not their depth or novelty but their clarity and concision, their high degree of technical and performative polish, and Donen and cinematographer Harold Rosson's imaginative but naturalistic cinematography (within the limitations of slow, garish-by-nature Technicolor film and backlot sets). Aside from the ballet, every number is temporally economical if not actually brief. The film proceeds from one reasonably logical episode to another, generally quickly. There is much more to say about how the songs "work" in each of those positions. This leads us to the next chapter, focused on the invisible artistry of the MGM music department, which adorned Comden and Green's wisest cracks and Kelly and Donen's finest steps and shots in *Singin'* with inventive, subtle, satisfying musical arrangements, underscoring, and sound effects.

4

Music and Sound

> "He [Conrad Salinger] could translate colour and mood into sound
> to produce the most startling production numbers. When needed
> he could write on a grand scale, as in the climax of 'This Heart of
> Mine' ('Ziegfeld Follies,' 1946), and then he would paint delicate
> smaller scale sound pictures as in parts of 'Singin' in the Rain'
> (1952)."
>
> John Wilson

When Gene Kelly was asked by an interviewer who the important people
in the MGM music department were, he responded, "the arrangers. Conrad
Salinger was most important to the dancers, because he could do things with
the mood numbers."[1] Kelly also picked out Roger Edens, along with Saul
Chaplin, calling them "the translators, the interpreters" between choreographer and arranger.[2] After praising conductors Johnny Green, André Previn,
and Lennie Hayton, as well as "great musicians" and "dedicated motion
picture men," Kelly ended where he began, concluding, "I think the heroes
unsung were the arrangers. They did fantastic jobs."[3] In the quote above, contemporary conductor and movie music scholar John Wilson concurred with
Kelly's judgment.[4]

Arranging at MGM on a tight schedule necessitated division of skilled
labor. Multiple arrangers passed short scores with details on instrumentation
to multiple orchestrators. Copyists created legible copies of scores and parts
for the musicians. In a musical, the songs generally constituted the principal
musical materials the arrangers wove into a full score, along with original
musical ideas. Freed and Brown were successful songwriters, together and in
collaboration with others, for a decade before they joined MGM. Their songs
had already been repeatedly arranged and rearranged for a variety of forces
and voices.

Singin' in the Rain. Andrew Buchman, Oxford University Press. © Oxford University Press 2024.
DOI: 10.1093/9780197760062.003.0004

"OK," Go: Audio and Film Production Begin

Even before the "OK" script of *Singin' in the Rain* was approved by Freed on April 11, in March 1951 MGM's music department began to prepare for the film to enter production. New arrangements were commissioned for all the songs in the score. Roger Edens and Lennie Hayton spread the work out among a group of orchestrators and arrangers on contract with the studio. According to musicologist Todd Decker, Conrad Salinger was "Kelly's man at Metro."[5] Salinger arranged the main title music (the opening trio in raincoats and underscoring leading into the scenes at a movie premiere at the Chinese Theatre) and all three of Kelly's vocal solos: "Singin' in the Rain," "You Were Meant for Me" (including a dance duet with Reynolds), and his solo version of "All I Do Is Dream of You," later cut. Salinger also arranged "Make 'Em Laugh" for O'Connor. Decker has also explained how, frequently, Salinger set ballet sequences and Lloyd "Skip" Martin specialized in jazz dance arrangements on other films at MGM as well.[6]

Both arrangers and orchestrators are carefully credited in the liner notes accompanying the double CD release of the soundtrack published fifty years after the film's premiere, in 2002.[7] These notes distinguish between arrangers, who sketched out a given number, perhaps in a short score (just four staves of music), and orchestrators who translated each nascent arrangement into a full orchestral score. See table 4.1.

After arrangements were completed, audio recordings were made, before the scenes containing the songs were shot. Although ghost-singing is parodied mercilessly in *Singin' in the Rain*, that's exactly what all the singers did to prepare the musical soundtrack. However, they generally ghosted for themselves. Performing the same songs on camera, actors then lip-synched to their own prerecorded audio tracks, played back on the set.

Dialogue was generally audiorecorded simultaneously with images. But it was also routinely subject to overdubbing to correct deficiencies due to random noises, microphone placement, or line flubs, a process sometimes known as looping. The disastrous attempts to record Lina's voice on the set are solved via looping. The two quasi-documentary re-enactments of looping sessions in *Singin'* are discussed below.

Debbie Reynolds, the only singer in the film with a hit single, possessing a promising voice that was still developing, was also the only performer whose voice was dubbed by a ghost singer.[8] Just as the plain-talking character Lina Lamont was saddled with a screen image as an aristocrat, Reynolds, who

Table 4.1 Specific Arrangers and Orchestrators for Musical Numbers
(songs by Freed & Brown unless otherwise noted)

Title	Arranger	Orchestrator	Duration	Date(s) recorded
"Singin' in the Rain"	Conrad Salinger	Bob Franklyn	0:01:17	June 5, 1951; December 12, 1951; & January 16, 1952
"Dignity" underscoring	Lennie Hayton	Wally Heglin	0:00:53	November 19, 1951
"Stunt Montage" underscoring	Hayton	Heglin	0:02:05	November 17 & 20, 1951
"First Silent Picture" underscoring	Hayton	Heglin	0:01:26	November 17, 1951
"Fit as a Fiddle" (by Freed, Hoffman, & Goodhart)	Heglin	Heglin	0:01:40	May 23, 1951; & November 20, 1951
Tango at mansion—"Temptation" (instrumental)	Lennie Hayton	Heglin	0:01:07	November 20, 1951
"All I Do Is Dream of You" (Reynolds & ensemble)	Heglin	Heglin	0:01:24	May 23, 1951
"All I Do Is Dream of You" (for Kelly; cut)	*Salinger*	*Franklyn*		*November 19, 1951; & December 12, 1951*
"Make 'Em Laugh" (patter by Edens)	Salinger	Salinger	0:03:38	June 22, 1951; & November 20, 1951
"Beautiful Girl Montage"	Roger Edens & Salinger	Franklyn	0:00:59	June 8, 1951; June 20, 1951; & November 19, 1951
"Beautiful Girl"	Edens & Salinger	Franklyn	0:03:17	June 8, 1951
"Have Lunch with Me" underscoring	Hayton	Heglin	0:02:42	November 20, 1951
"You Were Meant for Me"	Salinger	Franklyn	0:03:32	May 22, 1951; November 17, 1951; & January 16, 1952
"You Are My Lucky Star" (for Reynolds; cut; patter by Edens)	*Maurice de Packh*	*de Packh*		*June 13, 1951*
"Moses" (by Edens, Comden, &Green)	Edens	Lloyd "Skip" Martin	0:02:42	May 22, 1951; & November 19, 1951
"Good Morning" (patter by Comden & Green)	Heglin	Heglin	0:03:14	June 8, 1951

Table 4.1 Continued

Title	Arranger	Orchestrator	Duration	Date(s) recorded
"Singin' in the Rain" (reprise; Kelly)	Salinger	Franklyn	0:03:58	June 5, 1951; November 19, 1951; & January 16, 1952
"Would You?" (dubbed by Betty Noyes for Reynolds)	de Packh	de Packh	0:01:40	November 19, 1951; & January 17, 1952
"Broadway Ballet" ("The Broadway Melody" and "Broadway Rhythm")	Hayton & Salinger	Salinger	0:13:13	October 12–13, 1951; December 12, 1951; & January 16, 1952
"Would You?" (reprise; Noyes [for Reynolds] & Kelly)	de Packh	de Packh	0:01:08	June 5, 1951; & November 17, 1951
"Singin' in the Rain" (second reprise; Reynolds)	Alexander Courage	Courage	0:01:16	June 13, 1951; & November 20, 1951
"You Are My Lucky Star" (Kelly, chorus)	Salinger	Franklyn	0:01:37	June 5, 1951; & November 20, 1951
Total			0:52:48	

Source: Notes to *Singin' in the Rain,* 2-CD set of soundtrack and outtakes.

had often played an uppity younger sister in her previous supporting roles at MGM (and had a gutsy, chesty vocal delivery to match), was playing a guileless ingénue this time out. An uncredited ghost singer, Betty Noyes, lent the character Kathy Selden a lighter, more lyrical singing voice with near-perfect intonation in two numbers: both iterations of "Would You" and the "You Are My Lucky Star" duet with Kelly. All three scenes occur toward the end of *Singin'*.[9] Reynolds sang for herself in both her trio and solo versions of "Singin' in the Rain," in the trio "Good Morning," and in her cut solo version of "You Are My Lucky Star."

Later the music crew would also add underscoring—instrumental music to reinforce key moments of dialogue or action or provide a suitable accompaniment to dancing. MGM employed underscoring liberally in many of their nonmusical films as well and even employed an in-house orchestra. In 1949 the ensemble had been overhauled by music director Johnny Green; half the musicians had been replaced.[10] The orchestra became an emblem of prestige for the studio. which featured the ensemble in six short films released in 1953 and 1954.[11] However, even these specifically musical showcases were dubbed, a compromise made in order to portray the musicians playing on a grandiose set with few microphones in sight.[12]

During audio recording sessions in the 1950s before multitrack recording became common the orchestra and singers would be recorded at the same time. The orchestra visible in the background of Kathy's dubbing session for Lina's onscreen rendition of "Would You?" (discussed later) is made up of MGM's contract musicians who are also having to mime along to a recording made earlier, no mean feat. Although some live mixing between multiple microphones was possible, there was a minimum of multitrack recording in Hollywood at this time. Magnetic tape, a German invention, was on its way to universal adoption, but in 1951 Hollywood monophonic audio recordings were still made optically on film stock and sometimes transferred to acetate disks used for rehearsals, as had been the practice since the 1930s.[13] Silent images and the optical soundtrack were then synched and combined during the editing process.

Recording the Arrangements and Underscoring

In a memo dated March 22, 1951, music department head Johnny Green assigned composer Lennie Hayton to the film as the music director who would conduct musicians and singers in audio recording sessions. Hayton was also assigned authorship credit for most of the music cues for the film, even though most were largely created by others (see, table 4.4).[14] Two weeks later on April 4 a list of seventeen major music cues was circulated, transcribed in table 4.2.[15]

This table, drawn from an archived in-house memorandum, uncovers other materials cut from the film that may have existed, at least as scores, at some point. Nos. 3, 5, 6, 7, and 12 in the April 4 cue list were never used; cues 3 and 8 were filmed but cut, and cue 4 was edited down in post-production by two minutes. Among these unrealized ideas, the trio for Kathy, Zelda, and a third "girl," "We'll Make Hay While the Sun Shines," is something of a mystery, since no screenplay materials exist naming this number.[16] It was a topical choice, since it contains the line "we'll make love when it rains" and was first featured in an ambitious dream sequence ending in a thunderstorm, in *Going Hollywood* (1933), where it is first sung by Bing Crosby and Marion Davies, then by a female trio accompanying a rustic ballet set in a barnyard

Table 4.2 Tentative Musical Layout as of April 4, 1951

---

1. Interview ... DON AND COSMO — "Fit as a Fiddle" (1932)

2. **Kathy and girls at party**—"All I Do Is Dream of You" (1934) [Reynolds is inaudible]

3. *Don— after party—"All I Do Is Dream of You" [filmed but cut]*

4. *Don and Cosmo and [Ensemble on] Set—"Wedding of the Painted Doll" (1929) [edited down]*

5. Zelda—Kathy and another girl—Rehearsal— "We'll Make Hay While the Sun Shines" (1933) [never used]

6. Kathy's Audition [not used]

9. [formerly 7] **Don and Cosmo**—"Tongue Twisters" (1952)

7. [formerly 8] Don and Kathy on back lot—"Should I Reveal" (1930) [not used]

8. *[formerly 9] Kathy—"[You Are My] Lucky Star" (1935) [filmed but cut; Reynolds's voice]*

10. **Don, Cosmo, and Kathy**—Restaurant—"Good Morning" (1939) [Reynolds's voice]

11. **Don**—"Singing in The Rain"

12. Cosmo—"Piano Playing Pioneer" [not used]

13. **Kathy—Records for Lina** ["Would You" (1936), sung by Noyes and spoken by Hagen]

14. **Don's solo**—"Broadway Melody" (1929)

15. **Don and Lina**—Premiere Number [reprise of cut 13]

16. **Kathy sings for Lina at Premiere**—"Singing in the Rain" (1929) [Reynolds's voice]

17. **Don on stage at Premiere**—"You Are My Lucky Star" (1935) [Kathy dubbed by Noyes]

Source: "'Singin' in the Rain' Production April–July 1951," memo dated April 4, 1951, Arthur Freed Papers, Box 22, Folder 15, USC.

including a bevy of dancing scarecrows.[17] Some of the origins of the songs that did make it into the picture have equally illustrious pedigrees, explored further in table 4.3.

A number of music cues missing from this preliminary list were added during production, including the instrumental arrangement of the song "Temptation" (1933) by Brown and Freed played at R. F.'s party as the guests tango. Refer back to tables 2.2 and 3.4 to review such details. No. 4, "Wedding of the Painted Doll," a provisional choice for an unspecified duet included in the first draft for Don and Cosmo clowning around on set while waiting for Lina to appear, was replaced by Cosmo's solo, "Make 'Em Laugh." No. 5, the one chance Zelda (that is, Rita Moreno) had to sing and dance, was cut, as was an audition piece for Kathy, No. 6. No. 7, "Should I Reveal?" was replaced by "You Were Meant for Me" by June 25, the date of the page on which it was inserted into working copies of the "OK" script. Added notes in brackets also note the numbers Reynolds recorded but on which her voice was replaced in post-production with overdubs by Betty Noyes or Jean Hagen.

While much of the piano music intended for Oscar Levant had disappeared by April 4, No. 12 was carried over in this list from Comden and Green's first draft. Tentatively titled *Piano-Playing Pioneer,* this was an over-the-top Wild West scene in which Levant was to forestall an impending battle between a wagon train of settlers and a mounted party of indigenous fighters by revealing a grand piano hidden in a covered wagon and playing some lovely classical music, inspiring a peaceful rapprochement.

As noted, O'Connor signed on to the film late in March 1951 after his studio finally agreed to allow him to receive the $50,000 they were charging MGM for lending the actor out to a rival studio. "It was the first time I ever rebelled in my life," O'Connor told critic Roger Ebert in 2003. "I said, 'It's wonderful, but I'm not going to do it if I don't get paid.' "[18] O'Connor got his signing bonus, and deleting *Piano-Playing Pioneer* saved the studio a ton of money. Eventually a solo number specifically for O'Connor was added to the story, "Make 'Em Laugh." However, the idea of a large production number, virtually a movie within the movie, was also retained in the form of Kelly's new "Broadway Ballet."

Rehearsals and Audio Recording Sessions

Dance rehearsals for Reynolds alone began on April 2, the day after her nineteenth birthday. Gradually other members of the cast began to join rehearsals. After more than a month of dance rehearsals, the cast spent several days in May audio recording the musical numbers. Shooting began on June 16, punctuated with many more rehearsals. Instrumental underscoring was recorded beginning October 19, including retakes of some of the accompaniments to musical numbers, carefully timed to match the scenes as shot.[19] Production formally concluded on November 21, although some scenes were picked up later along with sound-sweetening sessions to dub in additional audio elements such as the sound of shoe taps in tap dance sequences and more underscoring.

"Pre-recording"—that is, recording audio tracks to which the actors would lip-synch on camera—began May 22. That day Kelly recorded "You Were Meant for Me" and (with O'Connor) "Moses."[20] The next day the two men recorded "Fit as a Fiddle" and Reynolds recorded her version of "All I Do Is Dream of You," although her voice, mixed in with the ensemble, is inaudible in the finished film.[21] Both the opening trio version and Kelly's solo version of "Singin' in the Rain" were recorded on June 5.[22] On June 8 the trio version of "Good Morning" was recorded, then recorded again on June 13, along with retakes of "Singin' in the Rain." Reynolds also recorded her ill-fated solo version of "Lucky Star" on June 13 (eventually cut from the film).[23]

Listing these audio recording sessions underlines the labor and time that went into creating a Hollywood musical at the time. The sessions occurred weeks before the scenes were actually shot. The film was shot out of sequence, with the most strenuous and difficult dances scheduled first, while the cast was rested and uninjured. For example, the actual dance sequence for "Good Morning" was shot on Reynolds's first day on the set, June 23, ten days after the second audio session. After fourteen hours, her feet were bleeding but the scene was completed.[24] Filming for Kelly's solo dance in the rain was tentatively scheduled for July 3–5, but then rescheduled to July 17–19, more than month after Kelly recorded the audio track to which he lip-synched.[25] As explored in chapter 3, recording, rehearsing, and shooting the ballet, interspersed with rehearsals and other work, occurred over three months, between August 20 and November 21.[26]

Dubbing "Would You?" and Dialogue, Too—Illustrating the Process of Making a Musical

Singin' includes depictions of the processes of actual musical filmmaking, albeit dramatized and fictionalized to an extent. Looping is portrayed as elegiac, easeful, and romantic, the opposite of the comical portrayals of Lina's struggles with her own voice and with microphones. In scenes featuring the song "Would You?" each step in the process in the film, from making a master audio track, through rehearsing with the audio recording as it plays back in order to practice your lip-synching, to performing the ersatz act of singing as the camera rolls is depicted in the film.

First, we see Kathy recording "Would You?" in an audio session on a soundstage, with the MGM orchestra itself in the background (1:13:24). Comically, we hear Lina's attempts to sing along with Kathy's overdubbing (1:14:08). Matters improve as the scene dissolves to Lina lip-synching successfully along with Kathy as the slate is cracked and the camera rolls (1:14:24). We see the camera crew, then what the camera sees: Don and

Lina in love (1:14:33). The magic of the final result is revealed, as the screen dissolves from color to black and white (1:14:54). The camera pulls back again and we hear R. F. exultantly proclaim, "Perfect. That Selden girl is great" (1:15:11).

The mood of successful magic is renewed during a second looping session just for dialogue, after the "Broadway Ballet" concludes (1:29:04). Don declares his love for Kathy and even announces that he will go public with her role in the film. He embraces her and they kiss. Sadly, tipped off by Zelda, Lina walks in on the couple at that very moment, and a violent argument ensues. The film's narrative climax is well launched, as Lina hatches a plan to keep Kathy a nameless ghost singer in perpetuity.

Reynolds's speaking voice in this second looping scene was also dubbed, in this case by Jean Hagen herself—a double dub.[27] The decision to dub Reynolds's speaking voice in this scene may have been made by Donen, who had learned to mask his own South Carolina accent after he first arrived in New York as a teenager. He said Reynolds's voice "had that terrible western noise" (she was originally from Texas), a poor match for Lina's "cultured speech" in the scene.[28] In the first quasi-documentary footage of Kathy in the studio, both she and the musicians are lip- (or bow-) synching to their own previously recorded sounds. As mentioned, at a later date Betty Noyes then lip-synched to Kathy's filmed scene, replacing Reynolds's voice with her own. After production was completed, additional audio looping sessions were routinely scheduled to rerecord dialogue spoiled by technical issues or background sounds.

Although what we would now call multitracking was a laborious process, sounds could be replayed, remixed, and rerecorded in order to make fine adjustments to sound levels and to add elements that couldn't be recorded in advance such as sound effects. For example, the sounds of rain and feet splashing in puddles were added to the soundtrack of Kelly's famous solo song and dance. A live dancer would generally add the sound of taps to previously filmed tap dance sequences. The preliminary work on microphone placement and levels to get convincing "wet taps" was done by his assistant Carol Haney, working with audio technician Conrad Kahn (supervised by Lela Simone). Then, according to Dabholkar and Hess, Kelly dubbed in all his own taps, even the splashing ones, to complete the soundtrack for his dances and for Reynolds's steps in "Good Morning."[29] O'Connor also dubbed in his own taps.[30] Lela Simone supervised these final rounds of sound sweetening; the stars' taps were recorded by William "Bill" Saracino.[31]

Selecting from Brown and Freed's Back Catalog

Aside from the title song, according to Comden and Green Freed left the choice of songs for the new musical in the hands of the writers, assisted by Roger Edens.[32] Edens introduced Comden and Green to these songs by playing and singing them "in his Southern colonel's whiskey baritone," on the grand piano in his corner office next to Freed's.[33] Although Edens isn't listed in the credits, his participation as assistant producer was crucial. Edens met with Comden and Green regularly in 1950, working through a stack of past hits by Brown and Freed. Almost all of these had already appeared in one or more MGM films. See table 4.3.

Table 4.3 A Chronology of Songs in the Film *Singin' in the Rain* (1952), According to the Release Dates of the Films in Which They First Appeared. All songs are by Brown and Freed unless otherwise noted. Numbers added to the 1986 stage adaptation are included, marked with an asterisk (*). Numbers included on the 2-DVD release of *Singin'* as special features are marked with a caret (^).

"Broadway Melody,"^ "You Were Meant for Me,"^ and "Wedding of the Painted Doll" (February 1929, *Broadway Melody*)
"Singin' in the Rain"^ and "You Were Meant for Me"'" (June 1929, *Hollywood Revue*)
"Should I?" (1930, *Lord Byron of Broadway*)
"Fit as a Fiddle" (1932, released as sheet music; Freed, Al Hoffman, and Al Goodhart, co-authors)
"Beautiful Girl"^ (1933, *Stage Mother* in September and *Going Hollywood* in December)
"Temptation"^ (1933, *Going Hollywood*)
"All I Do Is Dream of You"^ (1934, *Sadie McKee*)
"Would You?"^ (June 1936, *San Francisco*)
"You Are My Lucky Star," "I've Got a Feelin' You're Foolin',"^ and "Broadway Rhythm"^ (September 1936, *Broadway Melody of 1936*)
"Good Morning"^ (1939, *Babes in Arms*)
"You Stepped Out of a Dream" (1941, *Ziegfeld Girl*) *
"What's Wrong with Me?" (1948, *The Kissing Bandit;* lyrics by Edward Heyman) *
"Make 'Em Laugh" (1952)
"Moses Supposes" (1952)

Sources: For material marked with an asterisk (*), 1986 Rental Script with Line Scores, Betty Comden Papers, Box 13, Folder 2, NYPL, unpaged. Songs by other writers were added to the 1983 London production. These included "I Can't Give You Anything But Love" (1928) by Jimmy McHugh and Dorothy Fields, "Too Marvelous for Words" (1938) by Johnny Mercer and Richard Whiting, and "Fascinating Rhythm" (1924) by George and Ira Gershwin.

For material marked with a caret (^), *Singin' in the Rain,* 2-DVD set (2002).

Regarding *Broadway Melody of 1936*, the film included performances of two earlier songs that would also reappear in *Singin'*: "Broadway Melody" and "All I Do Is Dream of You" (sung in French).

Previous Appearances in Films of the Songs in Singin'

With the exception of "Fit as a Fiddle," every old song in *Singin'* had already appeared in at least one previous Hollywood film. MGM even made three more films with the same title as Brown and Freed's first, Oscar-winning hit musical film, *Broadway Melody*.[34] As noted in Table 4.3, no fewer than five songs from the second film in the series, *Broadway Melody of 1936*, were reprised in *Singin' in the Rain*.[35]

Although none of the songs in the third film in the series, *Broadway Melody of 1938*, made it directly into *Singin'*, an aspect of a musical arrangement in that film deserves mention. Roger Edens wrote a new introduction and interlude and interpolated them into an arrangement of "You Made Me Love You" (1913, by Monaco and McCarthy). Retitled "Dear Mr. Gable" for the occasion, the song was performed onscreen by the fifteen-year-old Judy Garland as she stared at a framed photo of Clark Gable.[36] The new introduction Edens wrote for the cut solo number "You Are My Lucky Star" with Debbie Reynolds in *Singin'* was modeled on that for "Dear Mr. Gable."

The "doo-dee-doo-doo" riff Edens created for Kelly's solo rendition of "Singin' in the Rain" is another example of Edens's talent for easing a song into a narrative by adding a casual introductory recitative, couched somewhere between speech and song. In its original film appearance, no attempt was made to integrate "Singing in the Rain" into a larger narrative. *Hollywood Revue of 1929* is plotless, a sequence of loosely related skits presented on a proscenium stage with a curtain, thus taking on the trappings of a live performance, as do some early silent films.

"Singin' in the Rain" punctuated *Hollywood Revue*, appearing not once but three times in varied arrangements. The song was sung as a solo, a trio, and in a grand choral arrangement with orchestra in the two-color Technicolor finale featuring bevies of dancers in raincoats in simulated rain, set against a painted backdrop depicting a gigantic version of Noah's Ark.[37] The song's prominence may have been sparked not least by the opportunities its theme offered for spectacle: rain effects, backlit chorus lines of women and men in transparent and translucent raincoats on a grand staircase, and a mirrored stage.

Musical Styles of the Arrangements:
Updating the 1920s and '30s with Care

Many of Brown and Freed's songs set in a story taking place in 1927 were actually written in the 1930s, in the succeeding jazzier Swing Era. To be fair, some were written for movies set in the past and were deliberately archaic in style; this is true of "Would You," written for *San Francisco* (1936), a film set in 1906, where it is sung in operetta style by Jeanette MacDonald.[38] Earlier appearances of twelve of the songs are included as a fifty-minute special features on the 2-DVD release of *Singin'* (referenced in Table 4.2).

Arranger Wally Heglin (1902–1972) imaginatively relocated one of the songs explicitly into the 1920s. "All I Do Is Dream of You" replaced "You Are My Lucky Star" as Kathy's first number, performed just after she jumps out of a cake at R. F.'s after party celebrating the opening of *The Royal Rogue*. The song was a slow ballad in its early incarnations featured in films in 1929 and 1934. The key to making this substitution work was a musical transformation, a rearrangement of the song as an up-tempo, energetic Charleston, the signature dance of the 1920s.[39] In *Singin'*, the dancers also signal a Charleston by performing the knee-knocking gesture widely associated with the dance (23:40). Conrad Salinger complemented Heglin's work with a lush arrangement for Kelly of the song, this time once again as a mostly slow ballad, a cut number discussed in chapter 3.

This party scene begins with a sultry tango played by violins on the low G string, accompanied by a slapped bass drum. The melody is from "Temptation" by Brown and Freed, first sung by Bing Crosby in the 1933 film *Going Hollywood*. The song was released on a Brunswick 78 rpm record as well; Crosby was accompanied by none other than "Lennie Hayton and His Orchestra."[40] Hayton was also the music director on *Going Hollywood*.[41]

Hidden Features: Octave Leaps and Riffs in the Songs

While no doubt the primary considerations for the writers and directors were dramaturgical, the songs also share some musical characteristics. Several songs included in the score feature an octave leap prominently in the melody. Others repeat narrower melodic gestures three or more times, in effect making a rhythmic riff a principal feature of not just the song's accompaniment but of the melody itself.

Although an opening octave leap was "something of an Arlen trademark" in songs like Harold Arlen and E. Y. "Yip" Harburg's "Somewhere Over the Rainbow," an octave leap early on in a melody was also a favorite strategy of Brown's.[42] Unlike Arlen, Brown sometimes obsessively repeated the gesture, making his songs memorable but monotonous. "Singin' in the Rain" (the original title of the song does apostrophize the first word), begins with an octave leap, lending not just emphasis but exhilaration to the first syllable of the word "singing." The leap is then repeated six more times, on the subsequent ideas "I'm *laugh*[-ing at clouds]," "So *dark* [up above]," "The *sun's* [in my heart]," "I'll *walk* [down the lane]," "with a *hap*[-py refrain]," and finally to set the words "I'm *dancin'*." Kelly inserted the words "I'm dancin'" into the last line in the film; they don't appear in the sheet music, where the last line goes "And *singin'*, just singin' in the rain."

"You Are My Lucky Star" is even more emphatic in its use of octaves. The first three words are dramatized via leaps down, then back up an octave. "Lucky" hovers up high before the line plunges down an octave once again to the word "star." The entire melodic gesture (two octaves, a hover, and another octave) is repeated on the next words, "I saw you from afar." After an intervening section ending in a rising chromatic line on the words "I was starstruck," the three octaves recur, outlining the words "You're all my lucky charms" and "I'm lucky in your arms." As previously discussed, Freed's choice of the consonant-rich word "starstruck" is problematic to sing since it is placed at the high point of the melody.

Brown and Freed's "You Were Meant for Me," which appeared in both *Broadway Melody* (1929) and *Hollywood Revue of 1929*, was tied into the narrative with care, becoming "an early example in a long line of developments in which a song is written to further the plot of the story."[43] In an interview in the *Los Angeles Times,* Brown said that the director of *Broadway Melody*, Harry Beaumont, "wanted songs that carried the story and action beyond the power of the spoken dialogue. He did not simply fit songs into his picture for the sake of having music." At Beaumont's behest, they replaced one love song with a new one, "You Were Meant for Me," that "was just what the director wanted. He was quite right. The other song did not carry half the heart wallop in that particular scene as the new number did."[44]

Musical Example 4.1 Octave leaps in "Singin' in the Rain," "You Are My Lucky Star," and "You Were Meant for Me."

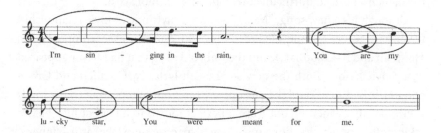

The song also underscores a fairly heart-walloping scene in *Singin' in the Rain,* Kathy and Don's adagio pas de deux. It, too, employs an octave leap between the words "*You* were" which drop down just a step. The melody then leaps down a seventh to complete the octave leap, on the word "meant." The line recovers from this leap, rising slightly again on the closing words "for me." See Musical Example 4.1.[45] Freed matches Brown's emphatic repetition of exactly the same melodic gesture with an equally emphatic reflexive reversal of the meaning of the first line, "*I* was meant [for you]." Less consequentially, after a chromatic interlude, the staggered octave leap is repeated twice more on the words [You're like a] *plain*-tive mel-ody," "[that] *nev*-er sets [me free]."

While it's certainly possible that Edens selected other songs on the basis of their intervallic similarities, in practice these seem to have no particular dramaturgical significance. Nevertheless, almost all the songs in the score contain prominent leaps totaling an octave. "Good Morning" and "Should I" begin with the same two intervallic leaps: first down a minor third, then up a major sixth, thus spanning an octave via an in-between note. "Broadway Rhythm" lingers incessantly on a single syncopated pitch, then launches itself upward through four intervening pitches to a high note an octave above.

"Broadway Melody" steps up on an upbeat to a starting pitch, launches upward through four notes and overshoots the octave by a third, then recovers, sinking back down to the octave above; the octave lies between the first word and the last syllable, as underlined and italicized here: "*Don't* bring a frown to old Broad-*way*." "*I've Got* a Feel-in' You're *Fool*-in'" uses an analogous gesture, repeating one note, then the note above it, then leaping up to the note an octave above the starting pitch, ending with a small leap back down on the syllable "-in." Spanning a smaller interval, but still leaping around, "All I Do Is _Dream_ of You" outlines the tonic triad in upward leaps spanning a minor third, then a perfect fourth, together equaling a minor sixth.

Although it's a new song, "Moses" shares a rhythmic motivic relationship to "Fit as a Fiddle," the only old Freed song with music by other composers (Al Hoffman and Al Goodhart), and the only old song that had never appeared in a movie before. Both the new song (with lyrics by Comden and Green and music by Edens) and the one one are built out of repeating (but varied) rhythmic riffs, widening out from a perfect fourth to a perfect fifth before taking off in other directions including a span of an octave, as it happens, between the underlined words "Fit as a fid-dle and _rea-dy_ for love."[46] The melody for "Moses" circles incessantly around one pitch, hiccups upward at the end of the first line ("are ros-es"), then dithers downward before settling on the second degree of the scale ("er-ro-ne-ous-ly"), a pattern made possible by Comden and Green's steady patter of amphibrachs (short-long-short poetic feet). See Musical Example 4.2.

"Moses" deserves special attention not only because it is a new composition but because of Lloyd "Skip" Martin's sizzling orchestration full of heart-stopping brass stabs, elegant countermelodies, brass and reed sections trading propulsive riffs, suspenseful moments of stop time, and a rush of changes in tempo and key toward the end. Was Edens trying to make it sound like another old Freed and Brown song, something like "Fit as a Fiddle," or was he attempting to bring the score a bit more up to date? It's rather different—more complex harmonically and more insistent in its use of riffs than "Fiddle."

Comden and Green's multisyllabic lyrics are something of a tour-de-force, combining Ira Gershwin-esque malapropisms like "Moses supposes his toeses are roses" with the clever internal rhyme in "erroneously"

Musical Example 4.2 Riffs in "Fit as a Fiddle" and "Moses."

and bright floral inventions like a "taffy daffy dilly," suggesting a mouth-watering daffodil crafted out of soft yellow candy. Martin rises to musical heights as well, with free counterpoint in the bridge more in the style of an on-the-beat piano exercise than swing band–style interlocking syncopated riffs. The two singers are thus musically pitted against one another, followed by a sudden wild modulation to a remote key (A-flat) and a return to unison chanting by both singers of a deliberate misquotation of Gertrude Stein's famous automatic phrase "a rose is a rose is a rose." See Musical Example 4.3.

The famous "doo dee doo doo" hum that launches Kelly's solo version of "Singin' in the Rain" is also a riff, made up of two exact repetitions followed by a slight variation. See Musical Example 4.4. Kelly attributed its creation to Edens, but the riff is not entirely original.[47] Brown built the instrumental introduction of the 1929 sheet music for the song out of a very similar riff, then included it again as an optional piano part during the second repeat of the chorus, marked "optional rain effect." The instrumental introduction to the sheet music is also unusually complex harmonically, moving through four chromatic chords (e^4_3–c^4_2–e-flat$^4_2$–D^{13}) in four measures, an unusual, impressionistic progression. Each of the four measures features a dancing melodic figure in the treble very close to the famous "doo-dee-doodoo" riff Kelly attributed to Edens, also reproduced in Musical Example 4.4.[48]

Musical Example 4.3 Free counterpoint and remote modulation in "Moses."

Musical Example 4.4   Riffs in the accompaniment to "Singin' in the Rain" in the 1929 sheet music and the 1952 film score.

After the familiar 32-bar chorus, a contrasting 24-bar-long B section in the minor mode moves through a series of remote keys, setting words including the plaintive, feel-bad questions "Why am I smilin' and why do I sing?" The following repeat of the chorus back in major mode includes an ad libitum contrapuntal part for the pianist that also features the opening riff, discussed earlier. This final fillip is described as an "Optional rain effect," also included in Musical Example 4.4. All three performances of "Singing in the Rain" in *Hollywood Revue* as well as the sheet music version of the song published in 1929 include the contrasting section in the minor mode and the second chorus, both omitted from arrangements in the 1952 film.

While Brown may well have devised these harmonies and counterpoint, in a profile published in 1927 in the *Los Angeles Times* he claimed he didn't bother himself with such details. "Brown, like Irving Berlin, does not use his technical knowledge of music in composing piano numbers. When a melody comes to him, he passes it on to an arranger who turns out the piano number as well as the orchestral arrangement."[49]

The most controversial song in the score remains Freed and Brown's shockingly close modification of Cole Porter's "Be a Clown" from *The Pirate* (1948) into a vehicle for Donald O'Connor, "Make 'Em Laugh."[50] If, as Carol Clover has stated, *Singin'* is an "object lesson on giving credit where credit is due," Freed and Brown's appropriation of "Be a Clown" is a glaring exception.[51] Michael Feinstein has called it "one of the most notable plagiarisms ever committed," and Donen said Irving Berlin confronted Freed about it at the time, to no avail.[52] Jonas Westover has published a detailed, note-by-note comparison of the two songs and the film scenes they accompany, discussed further in chapter 5.[53]

The opening rhythm of the two songs is similar: two shorter notes on an upbeat, followed by a long note on a downbeat, lending emphasis to the last syllable of an anapest. Porter repeats the rhythm three times in the first line, also repeating the title of the song once before varying the phrase: "Be a clown, be a clown; all the world loves a clown." Notice that although the contour of the first half of the line, up-down, is also repeated, Porter's repetition is varied. The first and fourth (last) emphasized syllables both land on the third degree of the song's tonic or home chord (the note E), descending an octave. See Musical Example 4.5.

In Brown's remix of this first gesture the starting pitch is longer, descends to a neighbor note, then is repeated, making the anapest (a short-short-long poetic foot) into an even more urgent cretic (long-short-long), something Freed picked up on with his choice of the action verb "make" and his elimination of the difficult diphthong "th" in the succeeding word. In the sheet music the first syllable of the melody is mildly syncopated, set on the second, weak beat of a fast duple meter (2/2 cut time in the sheet music, written out here in 4/4 for easier comparison).[54]

In performance O'Connor consistently syncopates the first note further, singing it a little ahead of the second beat and making the whole thing swing. While O'Connor managed to vary the melody a little further away from Porter's original, the two songs are also nearly identical in overall form. Both opening choruses are succeeded by a succession of verses made up of advisory lists of desirable clown attributes and their antitheses (such as being a dentist, in "Be a Clown," or a doctor, in "Make 'Em Laugh"). Both songs wind up with codas consisting of three repetitions of the title, set to varying bits of melody.

Musical Example 4.5 Comparison of the first lines of "Be a Clown" and "Make 'Em Laugh."

Underscoring and the Continuity Script

As mentioned in previous chapters a continuity script dated March 17, 1952, compiled during post-production to document the final cut of the film, provides a reliable source of the changes that took place after July 20, the latest date on pages inserted into the second "OK" draft dated April 11, 1951. The first page of the continuity script makes no reference either to Comden and Green or to being a script; yet recall that it was apparently the basis of much of the screenplay as published in 1972, along with new versions of staging directions derived directly from the film. It is titled simply "SINGIN' IN THE RAIN / (Dialogue Cutting Continuity)." Under the title Adrienne Fazan's name is listed, suggesting that she may have been the principal editor of this document, perhaps working with a continuity department scribe as the reel-by-reel editing was completed.[55]

The continuity script omits all set and acting directions in favor of technical information on shot numbers, camera angles (including approximate distance from the actors), footage, and even the number of film frames used in quick edits. Fazan used abbreviations for camera movements like MCS and LS for Medium Close-up Shot and Long Shot, TRUCK (a manly synonym for "dolly"), and PAN. Fazan noted "b.g." when describing action in the background of a given scene such as the entrance of another character, and "o.s." when describing sound or action off screen such as applause.[56] In the same folder preserved at the Academy Library reside several appendices: a full list of music cues (transcribed in table 4.4), including their authors of record; a revised version of the same list with timings for each musical excerpt created by the music department; and a copy of eleven pages of notes dated October 20, 1951, from Simone (the uncredited sound supervisor), addressed to the technical crew regarding adjustments to both music and sound effects.[57]

The music cue list contains the final versions of all eighty musical arrangements (including multiple sections within the "Broadway Ballet"), both with and without vocal tracks. This document gives a final account of where we began in table 4.2, with the much shorter list of prospective major cues needed for the pre-production audio recording sessions. The process of editing the film and adding in all these additional music cues began during production, while portions of the film were still being shot. See table 4.4.

Principal photography (except for the ballet) was completed by August 18, and Donen and Fazan finished a rough cut of this film footage on September

Table 4.4 Transcription of Final List of Music Cues with Authors of Record

SINGIN' IN THE RAIN		PROD. #1546	
[TITLE	COMPOSER(S)	PUBLISHER(S)	TIMING]
REEL 1			
1. SINGIN' IN THE RAIN	BROWN: FREED	ROBBINS	0:38
2. YOU ARE MY LUCKY STAR	"	"	0:48
3. DIGNITY	HAYTON		0:50
4. HARMONICA IMPROVISATION	[blank]		0:12
5. FIT AS A FIDDLE	HOFFMAN & GOODHART: FREED	FEIST	0:08
6. BURLESQUE	HAYTON		0:16
7. FIT AS A FIDDLE	HOFFMAN & GOODHART: FREED	FEIST	1:39
8. SUNNY CALIFORNIA	HAYTON		0:18
REEL 2			
9. SUNNY CALIFORNIA	HAYTON		0:08
10. STUNT MONTAGE	"		1:02
11. "	"		0:15
12. STUNT MONTAGE - PART 2	"		0:16
13. 1st SILENT PICTURE	"		1:16
14. GENE IS MOBBED	"		0:16
REEL 3			
15. KATHY ARRIVES AT THE PARTY	HAYTON		0:24
16. TEMPTATION	BROWN: FREED	ROBBINS	1:02
17. FANFARE	[blank]		0:04
18. ALL I DO IS DREAM OF YOU	BROWN: FREED	ROBBINS	1:25
19. THE PIE	HAYTON		0:19
REEL 4			
20. GENE DREAMS OF KATHY	HAYTON & SALINGER		0:28
21. DRUMS	[blank]		
22. PIANO IMPROVISATION	[blank]		
23. MAKE 'EM LAUGH	BROWN: FREED	ROBBINS	3:09

(*continued*)

Table 4.4 Continued

SINGIN' IN THE RAIN		PROD. #1546	
[TITLE	COMPOSER(S)	PUBLISHER(S)	TIMING]
REEL 5			
24. MINUET - "DON GIOVANNI"	MOZART	PD	0:58
25. VOCAL IMPROVISATION	[blank]		0:04
26. "	[blank]		0:04
27. DON'T EVERYBODY	HAYTON		0:17
28. I'VE GOT A FEELIN' YOU'RE FOOLIN'	BROWN: FREED		0:12
29. WEDDING OF THE PAINTED DOLL	"	MILLER	0:04
30. SHOULD I	"	ROBBINS	0:09
31. I'VE GOT A FEELIN' YOU'RE FOOLIN'	"	"	0:05
32. WEDDING OF THE PAINTED DOLL	"	MILLER	0:02
33. SHOULD I	"	ROBBINS	0:04
34. I'VE GOT A FEELIN' YOU'RE FOOLIN'	"	"	0:02
35. WEDDING OF THE PAINTED DOLL	"	MILLER	0:02
36. SHOULD I	"	ROBBINS	0:06
37. BEAUTIFUL GIRL	"	"	**3:15**
REEL 6			
~~38. ALL I DO IS DREAM OF YOU~~	~~BROWN: FREED~~	~~ROBBINS~~	~~1:51~~
39. THE STAGE IS SET	HAYTON		1:06
40. YOU WERE MEANT FOR ME	BROWN: FREED	ROBBINS	3:32
41. DICTION COACH	HAYTON		0:12

SINGIN' IN THE RAIN		PAGE 2	
REEL 7			
42. MOSES	EDENS, COMDEN, & GREEN	ROBBINS	2:40
43. SOUND WIRING	HAYTON		0:05
44. CUT	"		0:05
45. NEWS OF THE DAY - MAIN TITLE	ROCCHETTI	SAM FOX	0:10
46. TALKIE PREVIEW	HAYTON		0:26

Table 4.4 Continued

SINGIN' IN THE RAIN		PROD. #1546	
[TITLE	*COMPOSER(S)*	*PUBLISHER(S)*	*TIMING]*
REEL 8			
47. FIT AS A FIDDLE	HOFFMAN & GOODHART: FREED	FEIST	0:06
48. INTRO. "GOOD MORNING"	HAYTON		0:59
49. GOOD MORNING	**BROWN: FREED**	**CHAPPELL**	**3:15**
50. LA SORELLA	BOREL-CLERC	PD US; DEISS	0:04
51. GOOD MORNING	BROWN: FREED	CHAPPELL	0:18
REEL 9			
52. ALL I DO IS DREAM OF YOU	BROWN: FREED	ROBBINS	0:34
53. SINGIN' IN THE RAIN	**"**	**"**	**4:14**
54. FROM DUELING TO DANCING	HAYTON		0:48
55. "	"		0:09
56. WOULD YOU	**BROWN: FREED**	**ROBBINS**	**1:46**
REEL 10			
57. BROADWAY MELODY	**BROWN: FREED**	**ROBBINS**	**0:42**
58. BROADWAY BALLET-PART 1B	**HAYTON**		**0:57**
59. BROADWAY BALLET-PART 1C	**"**		**0:26**
60. BROADWAY RHYTHM	**BROWN: FREED**	**ROBBINS**	**0:02**
61. "	"	"	0:02
62. "	"	"	0:03
63. BROADWAY BALLET-PART 1C cont'd REVISED			
	HAYTON		0:16
64. BROADWAY RHYTHM	**BROWN: FREED**	**ROBBINS**	**1:50**
65. BROADWAY BALLET - PART 3 REV.	**HAYTON**		**0:52**
66. BROADWAY RHYTHM	**BROWN: FREED**	**ROBBINS**	**1:56**
67. BROADWAY BALLET - PART 4 INTRO. REV			
	HAYTON		0:12
68. BROADWAY RHYTHM	**BROWN: FREED**	**ROBBBINS**	**1:30**

(continued)

Table 4.4 Continued

SINGIN' IN THE RAIN		PROD. #1546	
[TITLE	COMPOSER(S)	PUBLISHER(S)	TIMING]
REEL 11			
69. CASINO - PART 2	HAYTON		0:15
70. BROADWAY RHYTHM	BROWN: FREED	ROBBINS	0:55
71. BROADWAY BALLET - PART 5 REVISED	HAYTON & SALINGER		0:26
72. BROADWAY RHYTHM	BROWN: FREED	ROBBINS	0:05
73. BROADWAY BALLET - PART 5 REVISED	HAYTON		1:09
74. BROADWAY MELODY	BROWN: FREED	ROBBINS	0:28
75. BROADWAY RHYTHM	"	"	0:22
76. BROADWAY MELODY	"	"	1:09
77. ALL I DO IS DREAM OF YOU	"	"	0:26
REEL 12-A			
78. WOULD YOU	BROWN: FREED		1:32
REEL 12-B			
79. SINGIN' IN THE RAIN	BROWN: FREED	ROBBINS	1:20
80. YOU ARE MY LUCKY STAR	"	"	1:38

Source: SINGIN' IN THE RAIN (1952), 1952-03-17, Turner/MGM Scripts, Folder S-1242, AL. Complete script divided into six reels for "(Dialogue Cutting Continuity) / (Film Editor: Adrienne Fazan, A.C.E.)," stamped "DEPARTMENT COPY" and "FILE COPY." No number. This document comprises a full script, annotated with technical notes on shots combined, reel by reel. Various documents follow, including: "SINGIN' IN THE RAIN / (Feature) / (Music Report and Footage), March 15 [penciled in] 17, 1952." Then a music cue sheet is provided, with additional columns as follows. NOTE: sung and/or danced numbers are in added **boldface**; a number deleted after post-production but before final release crossed out.

6. Then the sound and music crews set to work recording underscoring and adjusting prerecorded musical numbers when necessary.[58] The first step in this process generally was "spotting," in which the director, film and music editors, and the composer screened the film and determined where each music cue would start and stop. [59] The music editor would then draw a "'streamer," or line, across two or three seconds of film and punch a hole in a frame of a working copy of the film. The streamers, followed by the bright flash of the punches, cued the conductor when to begin a given music cue or change tempo within a longer cue.[60] By following the streamers and punches the conductor could be sure to hit crucial transitions right on the button.

Sometimes the conductor would also use a click track, listening through headphones, but it was rare at this time for the musicians to hear the click track even if one was used; they followed the conductor's lead.

The action around sound cue No. 27 in table 4.3, "Don't Everybody?" is a good illustration of how underscoring cues often operate, suggesting to audiences what to feel or swiftly taking viewers in a new narrative direction. After R. F. urges Don to keep doing what he's doing, "just add talking to it," he lays out a possible ad campaign using the slogan "Lamont and Lockwood: They Talk!" (34:20). Lina responds in her least aristocratic mode, ungrammatically asking "Don't everybody?" Notice how sound cue No. 27 starts subtly fading in—Simone's doing. The cue begins with a simple musical gesture, nothing but three descending notes on a bassoon played against a held chord in the winds—yet the result is a palpable instrumental sigh, reflecting the dismay of the three men as they consider the contrast between R. F.'s fantasy of success and Lina's unsaleable street corner voice, despite her regal appearance in full costume and makeup (34:29).

String tremolos, brass fanfares, and cymbal crashes herald three sets of whirling newspaper headlines as we transition swiftly into the "Beautiful Girl" montage (34:34). At 34:42 the next sound cue, No. 28 in Table 4.4, introduces the first vocal presentation of "I Got a Feelin' You're Foolin'." We are off to the races: seven more sound cues in less than a minute. In a complex montage like this in the era of modern multitrack recording it is likely that the following medley of brief sound cues, Nos. 29–36, would be created in the studio via the magic of multitracking. At MGM, the orchestra, led by Hayton, recorded each tiny excerpt of song or music separately before they were wedged together by Donen, Fazan, and the rest of the image and sound-editing crew. Writing out every note meant that musical effects could be crafted in, like the slowing tempo in cue No. 36 (at 35:25) leading smoothly into the slower extended song "Beautiful Girl."

Simone's decision to fade into the "Don't Everybody?" music cue rather than beginning it at full volume was one of dozens of judicious adjustments to dialogue, music, and sound effects she ordered during post-production. An eleven-page-long list of "Music Notes" appended to a copy of the continuity draft script housed at the Academy Library provides highlights of Simone's invisible but exquisitely audible contributions to the finished film.[61] Although many of the notes simply document edits probably determined during the "spotting" process, Simone also specifies sonic adjustments, such as "sweetening"—in this case, making more audible—Don and Cosmo's putative instrumental parts (on violin and piano, respectively) during the dance band scene in a saloon during the double autobiography. At another point Simone simply asks Hayton to "redo ending of 'Moses,'" trusting in the music crew to know what she's talking about. See table 4.5.

Listening to "Good Morning"

Memorable as it is, Kelly's solo rain dance is the tailpiece to the energetic and inventive trio "Good Morning." As mentioned earlier, he had swung down a backlot street and dickered with a cop with Rita Hayworth and Phil Silvers in *Cover Girl*. Kelly had also previously made Frank Sinatra leap over furniture—a series of bunk cots in a barracks—in *Anchors Aweigh*. The furnishings the trio used as dance props in "Good Morning" included "the original 1927 art deco furniture designed for the Greta Garbo/John Gilbert film *Flesh and the Devil*," unearthed for the occasion by set designer Jacque Mapes.[62]

The number begins with a brief a cappella reprise of "Fit as a Fiddle" by Cosmo alone, running himself into the kitchen wall in an attempt to cheer up Don, who's just admitted that his acting has been mannered, stilted, "a close second" to Lina's (1:00:44). Warm clarinets and rising violas signal a change in the air as another inventive arrangement by Wally Heglin begins (1:00:50). A mournful English horn playing in minor mode echoes Don's gloomy thoughts, until Kathy suggests making *The Dueling Cavalier* into a musical. A flute enters the mix, and the mode turns to major as the strings speed up their kinetic figuration (1:00:58). The orchestra gathers speed and energy as the characters scheme and Don declares "*The Dueling Cavalier* is now a musical!" (1:01:29). A horn call and high string tremolo sound as Kathy, perhaps channeling the pastoral bliss of the opening of *Oklahoma!*, proclaims, "and what a lovely mornin'!" (1:01:43).

The trio stride, singing, from the spacious kitchen on through Kelly's grand but cozy celebrity cottage filled with all that semi-antique furniture. On the bridge (or middle eight) the lines are divided up among the three performers unpredictably, so that we hear sometimes one, sometimes two, then all three voices in unison. Kathy adds a vocal obbligato, "and you, and you, and you, and you" after the first time through (1:02:23). The music modulates downward a minor third from B-flat to G major, and for a while the arrangement is perfectly suited to Reynolds's gutsy chest register. She

Table 4.5 Synopsis of Lela Simone's "Musical Notes"

"SINGIN' IN THE RAIN"
Production 1546
Music Notes

Reel 1

From Lion into studio click track for vocal "Singin' in the Rain" - sixteen bows. The click track will start from the first frame of the Lion on - lose clicks for remaining portion of title - lose music on fade into picture.

Start music on cue: "Well, Dora - dignity" etc. - continue scoring up to downbeat of Fit as a Fiddle. The pool room, the burlesque theater and the cafe will be done to click track. We will lose the clicks on the dissolves from town to town (COYOTE-VILLE).

Sweeten Fiddle track in number - make musical sound effects.

Music on dissolve to sunny California - get into hurry music - finish as first double falls into spittoon.

Reel 2

Start music at beginning of Gene in western costume. Continue scoring through stunts - throughout scene with producer and Lina - throughout billboards and finish just ahead of "Thank you, Don" (Gene's gesture).

Music on dissolve to theater - finish with cut off of orchestra leader.

Record exit march for backstage scene - finish with Jean Hagen's exit - start music as Gene runs to streetcar and finish as cop enters scene.

Reel 3

Start music as Gene's coat rips - through dissolve to party. Continue until producer says "Hold it" (use TEMPTATION). The foregoing scene will be done to click track.

Record fanfare at end of Simpson's speech: as Kathy comes out of cake.

Start in production to number (ALL I DO IS DREAM OF YOU) on cut to girls - meet downbeat of first chorus. This also will be done to click track.

Music as Kathy throws cake to end of reel.

Reel 4

Make piano track for Cosmo (Ahead of MAKE 'EM LAUGH).

As Donald jumps off piano record zip into Donald's vocal - Frankie Carlson: Make effects.

Reel 5

Make mood music for Cosmo.

As Director says "Cut" start music - into Mammy bit.

Start music after Jean Hagen's close up through inserts into BEAUTIFUL GIRL Montage.

(continued)

Table 4.5 Continued

BEAUTIFUL GIRL:

I

Orchestra track for end of first chorus.

II

Fashion show to existing piano track.

III

Orchestra track for end of number.

Reel 6

Start music as Donald leaves Kathy and Don on shooting stage - score through entire scene up to where Gene looks around.

Start music again on cut to dark stage (interior). Continue up to downbeat of verse YOU WERE MEANT FOR ME.

Re-do end of number up to off scene voice.

Reel 7

Start music on Kathy's hesitation after number - finish as lights go out.

SEGUE

Music as Kathy is running past billboard into downbeat of verse to LUCKY STAR.

Music of insert: DICTION COACH - finish inside studio - fade into dialogue.

Re-do ending of MOSES.

Reel 8

Short bridge on dissolve to sound wiring.

Short bridge as Director yells "Cut" - through Michael being placed on shoulder - lose in dialogue.

Score main title for talking picture up to first cut to Lina.

Possibly record Metro newsreel music for exterior of theater.

Reel 9

Start music as Donald runs into kitchen door - continue up to downbeat of Good Morning (throughout Kathy's upbeat).

Lennie: Make steel guitar and ukelele [sic] sweetener. [sic--"sweeter"?]

Reel 10

Music as Donald falls on sofa seat. Continue through dissolve to D on and Kathy in doorway - finish as Don stops on stairs.

SEGUE

Click track from where Gene stops on stairs into downbeat of vamp SINGIN' IN THE RAIN number. The foregoing scene will be done to click track.

Table 4.5 Continued

Make xylophone for umbrella on gate in RAIN number.

Music as Simpson walks toward camera - catch all dialogue and action cues - fade music into Intro of WOULD YOU.

Note: Reel 11 will be BROADWAY MELODY.

Reel 12

Start music on cut to Don and Kathy in looping room - finish on "There," Zelda yelling off scene.

Reel 13

Start music of close up of Lina through dialogue scene on screen into WOULD YOU.

Score dialogue insert in WOULDYOU. [sic]

Record new introduction for Intro to SINGIN' IN THE RAIN.

Record chorus track for end title.

---

even adds a simple melisma or two to the second chorus, as the men add new patter penned by Comden and Green, "nothing could be grander than to be in Lou'siana" and "might be just as zippy if we wuz in Mississippi"[63] (1:02:31 and 1:02:41). Kathy gets the second middle eight, then the men yell rather than sing "good mornin'!" in the last line of the second chorus (1:02:51).

As the music modulates upward and the tempo increases, more new patter in multiple languages is heard, including "good morning" in French, Spanish, German, Italian, Russian, and polyglot New Yorkish ("Mon Sewer" and "Razma Schmorgen")[64] (1:03:00). We end up a fifth higher, in D, and faster, too, as the trio begin to tap and dance in earnest after striding straight toward the camera in the best Kelly manner (1:03:08). As Kelly put it, "The more you can go into the camera the more force you'll get, the more impression of a third dimension."[65]

The trio grab their raincoats and trade hats for the fourth chorus, playacting. Cosmo grabs Kathy's cloche. Worn backward, it becomes an orientalist version of a turban (see their respective hats outside the theater, at 55:28). Kathy gets Don's brown trilby, and Don ends up with Cosmo's trim grey fedora (1:03:38). By this time the band is rocking, saxes and brass trading quick riffs in vintage swing big band style (1:03:36). A side drum sounds and the orchestra drones as the violins play an uptempo version of "Turkey in the Straw" with a vaguely Scottish flavor as the trio twirls (1:03:39).[66] Using their raincoats as skirts, they do a quick can-can as the low brass play the second "walking" theme from the first section of Gershwin's symphonic tone poem *An American in Paris* (1928), reused by Kelly the previous year for the climactic ballet in the musical film of that name (1:03:43).[67] Pizzicato strings and brass blares mark the next bridge, as the trio use their coats as puppets, poking their heads out above them (1:03:53). A quasi-Hawai'ian electric slide guitar enters the mix as Kathy pretends to hula and the men make their raincoats into large ukuleles as Cosmo chants, crudely, "waka laka, laka laka, laka laka, la" (1:04:01).

As the fifth chorus begins, Don goes up on his toes and assumes the attitude of a toreador doing a *sevilla* while the orchestra pumps out a backbeat (1:04:07). Next Cosmo launches into a Charleston, accompanied appropriately by the orchestra, still riffing on and roughing up the melody of "Good Morning." Again the string and brass trade riffs on the next bridge (1:04:24), as the dancers leap over the grandiose wet bar and back, drumming atop it before using it as a ballet barre (1:04:31), to a Tchaikovsky-esque accompaniment including a celeste. A final shortened chorus leads to a few brass shouts as the trio charge through the house and over two couches, knocking one over before collapsing onto it to a final fortissimo bass drum stroke (1:05:03). The number is over, but the story moves quickly along. Next Cosmo has his brainstorm: substitute Kathy's voice for Lina's, via a dubbing process he illustrates, live (1:05:50).

Listening to "Singin' in the Rain"

Freed recounted his own origin story about the creation of the title song in an interview: "I'll never forget how Herb [Brown] and I got around to writing 'Singin' in the Rain.' He came to me one afternoon with the news that he'd just written a great tune for a coloratura soprano. He sat down and played it with all the classic trills. All I could think of was that a vamp in the bass and a few minor changes would give it the zip for some lyrics."[68]

This may be an inaccurate account, given that according to Eaton the dummy lyric at this point was not operatic but bluesy ("I'm laughing at the blues"—see below). But it is true that the song as published in 1929 employs more complex harmonies than Hayton's 1951 rearrangement. Hayton cut the song down to the chorus, and (according to Kelly, at Edens's suggestion) took the opening vamp Edens reportedly created for Kelly to hum at the outset of the song and wove it ingeniously into the accompaniment, over and over.

The recurring vamp Roger Edens reputedly invented for Gene Kelly to hum at the start of his solo performance of "Singin' in the Rain" may be right up there with the opening of Beethoven's Fifth in the world's inventory of instantly recognizable ear worms (refer back to Musical Example 4.4). But the way Conrad Salinger artfully reused the vamp, subtly varying and reshaping it in his accompaniment, provides an object lesson in the craft of film scoring.[69] Further sound effects sculpted by Lela Simone add veristic sonic details throughout. As discussed in the last chapter, Kelly and Donen paid close attention to the transitions between speech and song around the musical numbers they crafted, sometimes integrating them in several ways at once. See table 4.6.

The vamp appears in a rising sequence, as if coming to life, after the strings play the opening of "All I Do Is Dream of You" (at 1:07:05) as Don and Kathy say good night at the door to her boarding house. In the background of the entire scene, sometimes louder, sometimes softer, we hear, almost subconsciously, the soft sound of rain falling. As Kathy closes her front door accompanied by a bass pedal (at 1:07:35), a flute in its lowest register plays a distant version of the vamp, akin to the opening of "Westminster Chimes." We then hear the waiting car's motor start up on the soundtrack. The strings play the vamp once (1:07:39), then sit on one note while the winds wind chromatically upward, then quickly upward twice more in little flurries of notes as Don waves away his chauffeur.

As the car pulls away the vamp begins in earnest (1:07:47), in a rising sequence, sounding twice. Then the strings suddenly ascend, and Kelly begins to sing (1:07:54), humming a full version of the vamp three times, doubled by a xylophone in the orchestra. Next a stab in the orchestra—a punctuation point made by the brass and percussion section—marks the point at which Kelly stops, shrugs, and furls his umbrella. The camera moves in for a medium close-up. We then see a new shot showing Kelly's full figure once more but from farther down the street so that he can walk toward the camera.

As Kelly sings the first verse (1:08:15), the orchestra repeats the vamp eight times in a row with slight variations. As Kelly leaps up to the iconic lamppost, the strings sweep upward with him—a bit of unobtrusive Mickey Mousing, early 1930s-style. The camera moves in for a medium close-up as he embraces the lamppost, adding an emphatic "H" to the beginning of the line as he sings, "[H]and I'm ready for love." Again the camera cuts to another medium long shot from further down the street so that Kelly can keep walking toward the lens.

Table 4.6 Conrad Salinger's Musical Arrangement for Don's Solo Song and Dance to "Singin' in the Rain"

Time	Description
1:07:05	SFX: rain falling. Strings play the opening of "All I Do Is Dream of You"
1:07:35	Over a bass pedal low flute plays version of vamp, akin to the opening of "Westminster Chimes" 1:07:36 SFX: waiting car's motor starts up
1:07:39	The "doo-dee-ooh-doo" vamp first appears in a rising sequence
1:07:41	winds wind chromatically upward, then quickly upward twice more in little flurries of notes
1:07:47	vamp repeated in a rising sequence, sounding twice. Strings wind upward.
1:07:54	Don hums slightly varied versions of the vamp three times, doubled by a xylophone in the orchestra
1:08:06	orchestra stab—a punctuation point made by the brass and percussion section
1:08:15	Don sings first verse, orchestra repeats the vamp eight times with slight variations
1:08:27	strings sweep upward as Don leaps onto lamppost
1:08:42	second verse; muted French horn doubles Don's melody at first, then drops out
1:08:49	trumpet stab (fragment of vamp)
1:08:52	first violins swoop upward as camera booms into closeup of Don's up-turned face
1:08:56	winds repeat the vamp three more times
1:09:07	raucous high brass play the vamp twice
1:09:11	new lyric: "dancing in the rain" followed by jubilant nonsense syllables, then "I'm happy again."
1:09:27	pronounced syncopation in orchestra as Don notices Mahout woman in window, bows
1:09:31	another new lyric: "I'm singin' and dancin' in the rain." Horn doubles melody
1:09:35	high brass play vamp in downward sequence, modulating (changing key)
1:09:39	flute and English horn play the melody in unison as Don dances
1:09:57	strings leap up as Don kicks umbrella into the air
1:10:04	muted percussive sounds (xylophone ?) as umbrella strikes iron picket fence
1:10:07	low brass pick up the melody again while high winds play a lively staccato countermelody
1:10:12	quick chromatic run in high strings and winds as Don spins
1:10:20	slower chromatic run by clarinet and flute in unison; then they play melody
1:10:32	quick chromatic run *down* as Don is drenched under downspout; modulation SFX: water gushing from downspout

Table 4.6 Continued

Time	Description
1:10:36	brass play the melody robustly, accompanied by a drum-and-cymbal trap set
1:10:46	high strings pick up the melody with the *winds* playing the accompaniment SFX: feet splashing in puddles (to 11:11:17, where rain sounds resume)
1:10:51	violas step upward in detached notes as Don mimes tightrope walking
1:10:53	cellos play quick tremolos as Don kicks water in the gutter
1:10:57	chromatic countermelody in horns
1:10:04	brass ring out the melody as Don puddle jumps
1:11:15	all instruments drop out except for a single French horn holding a suspenseful, suspended note
1:11:19	modulation, slower tempo; winds with the melody, punctuated by glockenspiel
1:11:29	held chords under Don's recitation as he explains himself to cop
1:11:36	flutes and xylophone played with soft mallets, then
1:11:43	xylophone alone sounds three final repetitions of the vamp.
1:11:48	solo flute holds a suspended high note briefly; SFX: rain becomes louder
1:11:51	number ends with soft pizzicato (plucked) note in the strings; the sound of the rain fades
1:11:54	dissolve to a shot of R. F. knocking desktop with fist; SFX: fist hitting desktop

Source: Lela Simone, "'SINGIN' IN THE RAIN' / Production 1546 / Music Notes," October 20, 1951, Turner/MGM Scripts, Folder S-1242, AL.

On the second verse (1:08:42) a muted French horn doubles Kelly's melody, then drops out as Kelly stops, spreads his arms and legs, and lets the rain beat on his face, his eyes closed. The camera, on a crane, moves in for a tight close-up from above (1:08:55). On the next shot, the winds repeat the vamp three more times, then muted brass instruments play it once more, raising the level of musical energy. Kelly begins dancing while singing his own newly invented verse that begins with the words "dancing in the rain" followed by jubilant nonsense syllables, then the phrase "I'm happy again." After a pause filled with dance and a polite bow to the cartoon of the Mahout lady in the smoke shop picture window as the camera moves in for another medium close-up, he concludes the verse with another new invention, "I'm singin' and dancin' in the rain."

In the next shot the music relaxes, modulating downward as Kelly taps, using his furled umbrella like a dancing cane, and a flute and bassoon play the melody. As Simone completed the film's soundtrack, she made a note to herself to "Make [a recording of a] xylophone for [the sound of Kelly's] umbrella on [the iron picket fence or] gate in RAIN number [at 1:10:04]."[70] Four seconds later the music modulates upward again and a new musical idea is introduced: a staccato melody in the high winds above muted trombones, then flute and clarinets together (1:10:22) softly repeating the melody. Again the camera moves in for a close-up of Kelly as he drenches himself briefly under a downspout (1:10:35). The rain sounds change to the sound of rushing water.

On the next shot the camera crane rises high as Kelly spins across the street and the brass play the melody robustly, accompanied by a drum-and-cymbal trap set. When Kelly leaps delicately up to the curb, high strings pick up the melody with the *winds* playing the accompaniment for once. As Kelly leaps back into the street and splashes through puddles madly (1:11:05), the brass section picks up the melody. As the policeman approaches, all the instruments drop out except for a single French horn holding a suspenseful, suspended note (1:11:17).

A Look Back: "Turning Tunes into Money" during Freed and Brown's Apprentice Years

Before Arthur Freed and Nacio Brown joined MGM in 1928, they had already been writing songs together and apart for over ten years.[71] Both men made their careers on the West Coast—they related only at an angle to New York City's Tin Pan Alley, and their work seldom appeared in Broadway revues. Freed performed as a singer, began writing songs and publishing them during World War I, toured a bit in vaudeville, opened a music store in Seattle, spent time in Chicago and on the road, then became a theatrical producer in Los Angeles in the 1920s.[72] Working as songwriters based in Los Angeles in the 1920s, Brown and Freed witnessed the heights of the silent film era firsthand, working in proximity to the industry as the studio system was established during the decade.

In 1922 a *Los Angeles Times* headline announced that the "New Tin Pan Alley Is In the West." The following illustrated article profiled "Some Jazz Composers Who Are Turning Tunes Into Money" including Nacio Brown, "author of 'Coral Sea,' 'Make Me,' and 'When Buddah [*sic*] Smiles.'" In the same article Brown himself explained the business, stating that a "really big hit will average from $30,000 to $40,000 [$500,000–$700,000 in 2024 dollars] for the composers."[73] In 1924 an unsigned news article in the same paper proclaimed that "Freed is known as never producing a failure. Each of his songs has sold in excess of 1,000,000 copies, while his phonograph records have also achieved phenomenal sales." Freed's hits reportedly included "After Every Party" (1922), "Applesauce" (1922), "Peggy Dear" (1922), "I Cried for You" (1923), and "Cover Me with Kisses" (1923), a lullaby with both music and lyrics by Freed, "sung with great success by Mort Downey, with the S.S. Leviathan Orchestra," under the management of bandleader Paul Whiteman.[74]

Freed used his newfound wealth to begin a career as a theatrical producer at a 1700-seat auditorium equipped with a movie screen he leased in 1924 on the fringes of downtown Los Angeles at 730 S. Grand Avenue. He renamed the venue the Grand-Avenue Theater, then changed the name again to the Orange Grove Theater.[75] He also produced shows at the Music Box Theatre on Hollywood Boulevard.[76] It was here that ex-Ziegfeld performer Doris Eaton first sang the song "Singin' in the Rain," she said, in 1929's *Hollywood Music Box Revue,* which ran for seventeen weeks but closed before the film *Hollywood Revue of 1929,* also featuring the song, opened.[77]

Brown went into real estate with his royalties. An article in the *Los Angeles Times* in the summer of 1923 announced, "Mr. Nacio Herb Brown, the famous composer, is becoming increasingly interested in the business growth of Beverly Hills, and announced his intention of building a forty-room hotel building with stores and cafe on the ground floor."[78] But he also stayed active as a composer. In 1927 the *Los Angeles Times* described the background of Brown's latest hit, "The Doll Dance" (1926), written for Eaton to perform in producer Carter De Haven's revue, *Fancies,* at the new Music Box Theatre on Hollywood Boulevard.[79] According to the article, "Ninety recording companies have turned it into records and piano rolls. . . . Fifty thousand [sheet music] copies of the song have been sold in Los Angeles alone and . . . over a two-day period last week 20,000 records were sold."[80]

More Origin Stories: Doris Eaton, "Laughing at the Blues," and Anne Shannon Monroe's Book

As noted in chapter 1, Freed's first choice of a source to adapt into *Singin' in the Rain* was a 1927 play, *Excess Baggage.* The first act featured a number of songs being performed as background music, sifting down the stairs from the stage of a small vaudeville theater to the dressing room where the action took place. The songs in the 1927 Broadway production were credited to Ray Henderson, Buddy DeSylva, and Lew Brown (no relation to Nacio), but at least one piece by Nacio Brown was also in the show. The cast included Doris Eaton in what she considered "one of my best roles," because it included dramatic scenes as well as her performance of Nacio Brown's instrumental "Doll Dance."[81] During a visit with the Eaton family in New York that year Brown played a draft of a new song "two years before the final version appeared as 'Singing in the Rain' after Arthur Freed added his lyrics."[82] According to Eaton, Brown sang it with a dummy lyric (that is, an iambic line that could be rewritten by a collaborating lyricist later), "I'm laughing at the blues." This biographical connection offers another clue to why Freed was attracted to *Excess Baggage* before turning to Comden and Green for something new.

A proximate inspiration for Freed's new lyrics (and probably the reason the song's title was apostrophized) may have been *Singing in the Rain* (1926), a best-selling inspirational memoir of life in rainy Western Oregon by Anne Shannon Monroe. For a Seattle family like Freed's, Monroe's celebration of "this green-winter land, glistening in the rain" may well have been a topic of conversation, including passages like the one explaining her title: "If we . . . briskly set about discovering the riches that are all about us, I wonder if we won't all find plenty to set us singing in the rain?"[83] While *Singin' in the Rain* was in preparation the studio negotiated a copyright clearance with Monroe's publisher for MGM's reuse of the title.[84]

If Eaton's memory was accurate, the title song was the oldest of all the old songs pulled out of Freed's trunk by Edens and company, drafted in 1927. The imaginative musical ideas added in by Edens and Salinger inspired Kelly to make the dance that has become the centerpiece of his artistic legacy. Sadly, the newest song by Freed and Brown, "Make 'Em Laugh," appears to be a slavish homage at best and a shameless steal at worst. Yet even this unpromising material was made fresh by extra patter (by Edens), a sparkling arrangement by Martin, and once-in-a-lifetime choreography and performance by O'Connor, doomed to return to Francis the Mule before too long. Despite the voluminous bibliography that has grown up around the film, much remains to be discovered and discussed about the music and dance of *Singin' in the Rain*.

5

Reception History

"I was there watching the day they filmed it [Kelly's solo dance to "Singin' in the Rain"]. I was always there watching; I never left the sets, even when I was not in a scene."

Rita Moreno in *Rita Moreno: A Memoir*, 98

Finding and Keeping an Audience

The first part of this chapter examines the promotional campaign accompanying the film's debut in New York City, MGM's largest domestic urban market and the home of its corporate parent, Loew's, and early reviews at home and abroad.[1] A divide emerged in these early reviews between admiring assessments of the performances and disdain for the screenplay, which was variously dismissed as "impudent, offhand comedy," "stronger on mass appeal than on class appeal," and "less of a narrative than a series of skits."[2] Although *Singin'* was commercially successful during its initial release in the spring of 1952, in the 1960s and 1970s it began to accumulate special status among critics as perhaps the best of Kelly's films, or even "a Hollywood masterpiece."[3]

Scholars also began writing about the film. In the 1970s and 1980s Rick Altman and Jane Feuer examined Hollywood musicals including *Singin'* as collaboratively produced artworks within a genre.[4] Hugh Fordin's 1977 survey of Freed's films, the 1992 British Film Institute guide to the film by Peter Wollen, and a 2009 volume for general audiences co-authored by Pratibha Dabholkar and Earl Hess stand out in what has become a rich bibliography of works about Broadway and Hollywood musicals and their creators.[5] Many recent scholarly articles, some surveyed here, have offered new interpretations of numbers from the film, including discussions of issues around appropriation, race, gender, and ethnicity in takeoffs and remixes of scenes from the film.

Singin' in the Rain. Andrew Buchman, Oxford University Press. © Oxford University Press 2024.
DOI: 10.1093/9780197760062.003.0005

Marketing *Singin' in the Rain* as a film suitable for children helped make its first run successful. Over the next twenty years, the film acquired critical prestige as well. *Singin'* continues to reign in the public's mind and in most critics' assessments as an outstanding example of the Hollywood Golden Age musical film. But all artworks exist on contested, shifting cultural terrain. While the reception history of *Singin' in the Rain* as an autonomous artwork continues, its legacy is in the process of being questioned, elaborated on, and extended by other artists who have remixed elements from the film into new works.

Initial Marketing and Reviews in New York City and Abroad

During its first week at Radio City Music Hall *Singin' in the Rain* grossed $146,000 ($1.75 million) in ticket sales.[6] It "rang up nearly $1,500,000 gross in April [1952] at 25 representative cities covered by *Variety*, and finished first three times in the weekly box office surveys."[7] Although these figures are unreliable, multiple secondary sources state that the film made a profit during its first run, despite cost overruns due to the ballet.[8] Still in circulation after another fifty years have passed, *Singin'* is still making money. The film is now owned by Warner Bros. Discovery, a corporate descendant of one of MGM's archrivals, the studio founded by the four Warner brothers.[9]

The publicity staff at MGM had a crucial role to play in the film's reception history: finding an audience for the movie during its first run. Marketing new movies was a particular challenge in New York City, where new films and stage shows popped up and fizzled out nearly every week and brand-new television stations were busy flooding the airwaves with free alternatives. Good buzz generated in New York could resound across the country, one reason *Singin' in the Rain* opened in the city two weeks before its general release. On the morning of March 27, 1952, the day *Singin' in the Rain* opened at Radio City Music Hall, a 2/3-page display advertisement appeared in the *New York Herald Tribune*, "a Republican paper, a Protestant paper and a paper more representative of the suburbs than the ethnic mix of the city."[10] MGM bought a smaller, 1/4-page spot in the *New York Times* for the same advertisement.[11] The ad framed the film as a celebratory Easter holiday entertainment suitable for a family excursion into the city. (See figure 5.1)

Two photos of Kelly and Reynolds doing a step from the Charleston are pasted-up side by side in the ad, although such a scene doesn't appear in the

Figure 5.1 Opening Day Display Ad for "Singin' in the Rain," March 27, 1952.

film. To their left O'Connor comically plays a violin like a cello, wearing the checked suit from the number "Fit as a Fiddle." O'Connor appears by himself, not side by side with Kelly as in the film. Droll caricatures of leggy Radio City Rockettes, the hall's resident dance company since 1932, fill in the background. A stamp-sized publicity photo of Cyd Charisse and Kelly makes her stylized wedding dress with its vast veil look more like a prim white ballet leotard.[12] The images play up the chaste romance between Reynolds and Kelly, downplay the male duets which are certainly among the high points of the film, and minimize the impact of Charisse's revealing costumes in the ballet.

The advertisement lists five film showings beginning with a morning matinee, bracketing four stage show performances anchored by the Rockettes.[13] Contradicting its rainy title, ad copy describes the film as "the sunshine musical . . . silver-lined with song and dance . . . gay with love and laughter . . . perfect holiday entertainment . . . by the producer and with the star of Academy Award winner, 'An American in Paris.'"[14] Indeed, just a week earlier the Oscar ceremonies had been shown on broadcast television, which was proving to be a powerful way of promoting films as well as undercutting them. *An American in Paris* starring Kelly won in six categories, including the most coveted award, Best Picture.[15]

The same day, the *New York Times* published a list of films approved as "suitable for children between the ages of 8 and 14" by the Schools Motion Picture Committee of the National Board of Review, composed of parents and teachers. Despite the battle with censors around the "Broadway Ballet" discussed in chapter 3, *Singin' in the Rain* was on the list.[16] At the bottom of the page smaller advertisements extolled some of the myriad of movie choices a trip into the city could include. Few of those films were considered suitable for children by the Schools Committee.[17]

A revival house advertised Kelly and Rita Hayworth in *Cover Girl* (1944) and Rex Harrison in *Escape* (1948). Frank Sinatra performed live in between screenings of *Meet Danny Wilson* (which opened on February 8, 1952); it offered a fictionalized biography of a singer, played by Sinatra. Actor Tony Curtis was also making personal appearances at the theater opening his new film, *Flesh and Fury,* the very same day, March 27. Curtis played a deaf boxing champion who falls in love and regains his hearing.[18] Counting Curtis's opus, a total of ten films opened in New York during the same week *Singin'* bowed at the Music Hall, including *Murder in the Cathedral* and *Lilli Marlene* from England; *Anthony of Padua* and *Les Misérables* from Italy; *Los Olvidados,* a 1950 film shot in Mexico directed by Luis Buñuel released under the English title *The Young and the Damned*; the English-language version of a Franco-American comedy released in France in 1951, *Pardon My French*; and two more American features, *My Six Convicts* starring Millard Mitchell (who also played R. F. in *Singin'*) and a film noir directed by Robert Wise titled *Captive City*.[19]

At the same time Broadway was presenting an assortment of musicals, including a revival of Kelly's first star vehicle, *Pal Joey* (1940), this time starring ballet dancer Harold Lang.[20] *Call Me Madam* (1950) with Ethel Merman was in its last six weeks; Donald O'Connor would later co-star with Merman in the 1953 film adaptation. *South Pacific* (1949), *Guys and Dolls* (1950), and *The King and I* (1951) with Gertrude Lawrence (who kept playing the role for over a year until August 16, 1952, just three weeks before her death) were in the middle of long runs, as was the comedic play *Gigi* (1951) starring Audrey Hepburn, which ran from November 1951 to May 1952.[21] It would become the basis of Freed's last great musical film, released in 1958. An article previewing Truman Capote's first play, *The Grass Harp,* with incidental music by Virgil Thomson, also opening on March 27, appeared on the same page with the *New York Times* ad for *Singin'*.[22] To sum up the state of the market, the film had plenty of competition, warranting a campaign specifically targeting suburban families with children under thirteen, looking for a simple, safe Easter weekend outing in the big city.

Signposts in the Press to a Growing Reputation

Bosley Crowther's opening review of the film in the *Times* appeared the next day.[23] He described "its plot, if that's what you'd call it," as "impudent, offhand comedy" and complained that the film's title had nothing to do with the story. He praised Hagen's performance as Lina but described her licentiously as "the slut-voiced leading lady" and "the guttersnipe silent queen." Crowther approved of the musical numbers "in the liveliest Kelly-cum-all style," calling them "elegant" and "gay." O'Connor, he wrote, "had a jolly romp in a battering and bruising slapstick number ['Make 'Em Laugh'] and joins with the star [Kelly] in making 'Moses' a lively thing." Crowther complimented Reynolds for her singing in "Would You?" (on which she was dubbed by Noyes) but dismissed "You Were Meant for Me" as "a sweet lump of Technicolored sugar." The "Broadway Ballet" consisted of "eye-filling acrobatics against a mammoth production splurge [on sets and costumes]." Crowther added that Charisse "stepped out of nowhere" into the movie. Crowther did praise Kelly's "most captivating number ... a beautifully soggy tap dance performed in the splashing rain."

A week later, a brief second review appeared. Crowther defended his view that the title bore no relation to the film's story, while acknowledging readers who had written him to point out the connection to the song's debut in *Hollywood Revue of 1929.* The reference to readers' letters suggests that

Singin' was already sparking strong reactions among the general public. This time around, Crowther volunteered that "'Singin' in the Rain' kids an era and a style of film-production about as well as it has ever been done."[24]

In contrast to Crowther's first mixed review in the *Times,* on the same day the reviewer for the *Herald Tribune* strongly endorsed the film. "It is hard to describe in a short space all the assets of 'Singin' in the Rain'—its amusement is crammed in so tight that it bulges out all over the place," wrote Otis Guernsey Jr.[25] He, too, described the screenplay as "less of a narrative than a series of skits" but "with a solid foundation of humor," and singled out the ballet, "part lowdown and part dreamlike," as "a fascinating mixture of satire and moody loneliness."

After this first, positive review extolling the performances in the film published on March 28, Guernsey, like Crowther, also wrote a second review that appeared on April 6.[26] This time he upped the ante, putting the film on a par with more acclaimed predecessors. "Adolph Green and Betty Comden have dug much deeper into their imaginations than any lyrics could penetrate. . . . The book not only has novelty, it is also consistently funny, a near-perfect synchronization of verbal gags and sight gags strung together with the production numbers. . . . Like the two other most important milestones of Freed's recent career at M-G-M, 'Meet Me in St. Louis' and "An American in Paris,' the new musical defies any attempt to describe it in formula terms. A formula musical is precisely what 'Singin' in the Rain' is not." Guernsey's second review ran on the front of the arts section below a related illustrated feature, a tour of the MGM studio complex.[27]

On April 13 the *Herald Tribune*'s dance critic Walter Terry also reviewed the film.[28] Terry began with a provocative comparison. "For those who were left disappointed . . . by the recent performances of the Sadler's Wells Theatre Ballet . . . permit me to recommend a tonic. Go to the Radio City Music Hall and watch the buoyant, amusing, skillful and highly professional dancing in the new film." He observed that most of the numbers were "comparatively short and deceptively modest . . . but they are superb dances, none the less, and represent the most appealing choreography to come from Mr. Kelly. . . . They grow easily and naturally out of scenes and incidents." While he observed that "the accent is upon comedy or upon lightness of mood," he praised the fantasy in Kelly's duets with Charisse—"not only visually beautiful but utterly sensual"—and Kelly's "bits and pieces which satirize . . . early versions of the motion-picture musical." On December 28, 1952, Guernsey placed *Singin'* at number four on his list of the ten best films of the year, after

High Noon, Limelight, and *The African Queen* but before *The Quiet Man, The Man in the White Suit, Viva Zapata!, The Greatest Show on Earth, The Four Poster,* and *The White Line.*[29]

After its gala premiere in New York *Singin'* opened at more theaters at home and abroad. Some international reviewers also offered praise for the performers, doubts about the screenplay, and comparisons with other film musicals. Alex Barris in the *Toronto Globe and Mail* wrote that *Singin'* was "one of the best movie musicals we've seen in recent years. If *An American in Paris* rated an Academy Award (and we were among those who didn't think so) then this film should get a Nobel prize."[30] Barris singled out O'Connor for fulsome praise, predicting that he would soon be "a top box office attraction" due to his "marvellous sense of timing, his offhand delivery of lines, his wonderful clowning and singing and dancing." A reviewer in the *Irish Times* in Dublin, identified the picture as "Entertainment with a capital E . . . a colourful hunk of Hollywood history."[31] On the other hand, the film rated only a capsule review placed after longer reviews of *Venetian Bird, High Noon,* and *The Light Touch,* if before an even shorter review of a French import, *Edward and Caroline.*

The anonymous "Critic in London" for the *Manchester Guardian* was lukewarm, writing that both *An American in Paris* and *Singin' in the Rain* were "good films," although "neither is the equal of 'On the Town.'"[32] The reviewer faintly praised the film's "effective, if fairly conventional humour" and "unusually imaginative song and dance" but felt that "the action tends to stop and then start again," falling into "the usual separate compartments." On the other hand, the critic said Kelly "dances brilliantly" and constituted "the brightest hope of the American 'musical.'" No commercial harm was done; the film ran for four weeks in Manchester.[33] Four weeks was a good run for a Hollywood product at home or abroad; usually American films disappeared after that. For *Singin',* however, its first run turned out to be just the beginning.

Later in the 1950s television stations began broadcasting old movies, especially family-friendly favorites. *Singin' in the Rain, The Wizard of Oz* (1939), and *It's a Wonderful Life* (1946) among others began cropping up on television every year as seasonal attractions. Adjusting to this fortuitous turn of events and hoping to profit from the demand television broadcasts were now helping to create for revivals, in 1958 MGM began rereleasing some of its older features, including *Singin',* as "Masterpiece Reprints," along with new pressbooks containing suggestions for advertising copy and images, not just in the US but in the UK as well.[34] In addition to repertory theaters, which often showed double features at bargain prices, MGM's fresh prints devoid of scratches or other damage served an emerging market, nonprofit film societies cropping up mostly in major metropolitan areas including Berkeley, just across the bay from San Francisco.

Singin' was programmed twice during 1958 for screenings by the Berkeley Film Society.[35] In the society's promotional newsletter an anonymous reviewer (identified as Pauline Kael by fellow critic Ronald Haver) wrote, "This is just about our favorite movie musical of all time—a mad satire on Hollywood in the late 20's, carried out with wit and exuberance. It falters, just slightly, with a too-long love song in a deserted studio stage, and then, with a lavish, oversized Broadway Melody ballet. These faults mar the unity, but they don't seriously affect one's enjoyment of this delightfully malicious view of picture-making."[36]

Kael's best-selling collection of review-essays, *I Lost It at the Movies* (1965), was a much broader forum for her views. There Kael pronounced the film "just about the best musical of all time."[37] Comden and Green quoted Kael's judgment in their foreword to the version of the script of *Singin'* published in 1972.[38] What is usually lost in quotation is Kael's context: an attack on the praise heaped by other critics onto the film version of the landmark stage musical *West Side Story* (1961). Fellow critic Richard Schickel did discuss this important point in his review of Kael's book.[39] He defended Kael's comparison and shared her judgment that the problem with *West Side Story* was its "'seriousness'" (a word he placed in scare quotes), which he found pretentious in a musical. For Kael and Schickel, the film's family-friendly lightness was one of its key virtues. They argued that *Singin'* fulfilled genre expectations for a Hollywood musical while exceeding most (or all) others in craft, imagination, and quality.

Cultural tastemakers in New York began to tout the film. Reporter Eugene Archer discussed *Singin'* first in a preview of a retrospective of Kelly's films scheduled at the Museum of Modern Art in New York in 1962 in the *New York Times,* describing it as "generally considered his most representative work."[40] "Before the age of videotape, internet, and niche movie channels," one of MOMA's film curators recently wrote, films "curated at MOMA garnered an outsize importance," influencing other museums and film festivals.[41] Journalists, museum curators, and scholars began building a critical and historical discourse around the Hollywood studio era, including musicals, almost always singling out *Singin'* for special attention.[42]

Haver, a film historian and film curator, has noted that in order for a film to maintain or gain a wider audience it must be seen more broadly, not just on programs at museums, cinémathèques, or film societies.[43] In Haver's view, the advocacy of influential critics like Kael (and, as we'll see, Vincent Canby), "explains why *Singin' in the Rain* was ultimately elevated to the pantheon of 'great films.' However, inclusion in this category does not necessarily inspire the love and devotion of the mass moviegoing public."[44] Haver attributed the film's increasing popularity to "constant theatrical circulation and its frequent prime-time telecasts in the 1960s."[45]

On Thursday, May 8, 1975, *Singin'* began a one-week special engagement back at Radio City Music Hall. On May 4 Vincent Canby, film critic for the *New York Times,* issued a review that was a complete break with the skepticism of his predecessor Bosley Crowther in 1952, published on the front page of the Arts &and Leisure Section in the extra-thick Sunday Edition. He began teasingly by recalling several great moments in film history, then declared that *Singin'* contained "at least half a dozen" equally memorable scenes, "in a film that won no major Academy Awards and wasn't even listed on many Ten-Best lists for the year it came out (1952)."[46]

Canby called *Singin'* "extraordinarily exuberant, always youthful" and "joyously indestructible," a film that "works just as well today as it did 23 years ago. Maybe better."[47] Canby also noted that the film "has never been very long away from us. It turns up periodically on television and it's a fixture in any repertory program devoted to the Golden Age of the American film musical from the early forties to the mid-fifties."[48]

Following in the footsteps of others' skeptical comments about Comden and Green's screenplay, Canby trod lightly on the issue of integration (touched on from differing directions in chapters 2, 3, and 4), an aesthetic ideal for Golden Age musicals established by the success of Rodgers and Hammerstein's shows from *Oklahoma!* (1943) to *The Sound of Music* (1959). Canby called the film "integrated, but it's not all that integrated on the face of it."[49] He cited the ballet as an example. "It could be argued this number doesn't have to be in the movie, but that is to overlook the excitement and wit of the number that make it an integral part of the film we've been watching."[50] He ended by stating that the film "has nothing to do with nostalgia or with sentimentality. It is, simply stated, a Hollywood masterpiece."[51] In the Thursday *Times,* the film appeared in a list of "Places to Take the City Youngster."[52]

Scholars Step In

In one of the earliest unmistakable signs that the film had attracted not just decent audiences but discerning critics, the future film director Claude Chabrol published a review-essay on *Singin'* in the Parisian journal *Cahiers du Cinéma* in 1953. He argued that Gene Kelly was a directorial auteur comparable to Charlie Chaplin, while also lamenting that authorial films were "rare in this kind of production."[53] Chabrol called *Singin'* "from start to finish, absolutely and resolutely the work of a filmmaker."[54] He was perhaps the first, but certainly not the last film expert or scholar to consider the film a work of art that transcended its commercial origins as a fungible Hollywood commodity, as well as its initial marketing push emphasizing its utility as a light entertainment suitable for children.

The scholarly literature on *Singin'* has deepened and broadened as the years have passed by. In 2010 Gillian Kelly interrogated the extension of the label of cinematic auteur to Gene Kelly. She questioned the ways the term has been defined and misinterpreted and acknowledged that "Kelly repeated *himself* in film after film" (italics in original).[55] But Gillian Kelly concluded that Gene Kelly deserved the designation due to his "control, authenticity, and innovation in *mise-en-scène*."[56]

In 2011 Elizabeth Chin examined the "vilification and misunderstanding of the panther dance," a takeoff remixing Gene Kelly's "Alter-Ego Dance" from *Cover Girl* with his solo rain dance from *Singin'* created and performed by Michael Jackson in the short promotional film *Black or White* directed by John Landis and seen by many millions of television viewers the same year.[57] Chin defended Jackson's "dark and gritty exploration of the ugly racial reality in a society in which people assert that they do not see race," concluding that "the invocation of Gene Kelly's famous dance number[s] can be seen as a retaking of territory that Kelly himself had appropriated from the Black street-corner tappers who preceded him."[58]

Singin' in the Rain was the subject of an entire conference held in Salzburg, Austria, in 2013. A collection of papers from that conclave was published in 2014, including a study of dramaturgy and structure by Nils Grosch and Jonas Menze and a dissection by Ralph Poole of the gendered stereotypes re-enacted in the film.[59] Grosch published a follow-up article on intertextual dramaturgy and pastiche in 2021, briefly summarizing how the arrangements of songs in the film comprise "an intertextual musical matrix that consistently refers to the styles and song types of the 1920s" before moving on to discussions of other films.[60]

In 2014 Cristina de Lucas explored the connections between the lyrics of "Singing in the Rain" and Kelly's choreography, employing film scholar Richard Dyer's concept of a "utopian sensibility" in Hollywood musicals along with Janet Adshead's analytical methodology to explore how the choreographic motifs that typify Kelly's creation, including the "smile pose," "happy rotation," and the "child-like splash" combine to achieve (for most viewers) a beatific synthesis rather than a cloying sentimentality.[61] Also in 2014 David Ireland explored the incongruous reuses of the song "Singin' in the Rain" in the dystopian action films *A Clockwork Orange* and *Die Hard,* using Roland Barthes's concept of the denotative relationship between signifier and signified to explain the deep horror these reuses can inspire.[62]

In 2016 Jonas Westover offered a sensitive, sensible analysis of "the construction of humor" in the MGM numbers featuring "Make 'Em Laugh" and its model, "Be a Clown," by first comparing the structure and melody of both songs. While acknowledging Donen's view that the song was "a direct ripoff" of Porter's opus, Westover took a more nuanced stance, seeing "Make 'Em Laugh" as an homage as well as a steal. He pointed out that Brown "gently reshaped" the melody while (obviously, deliberately) "rarely deviating too far from the model."[63] He faulted Freed's lyrics for lacking "the subtle touch of Porter" but singled out the phrase "honkytonk monkeyshines" as "especially creative."[64]

Westover went on to discuss the dance and cinematography in detail, contrasting Kelly's "athletic and agile" clowning alongside the Nicholas brothers (Harold and Fayard) with Kelly and Judy Garland's slower, valedictory clown duet filled vaudeville gags that ends *The Pirate* (1948). After discussing these two differing settings of the song "Be a Clown," Westover interpreted "Make 'Em Laugh" as "a synthesis of the previous movie's separate takes."[65] In Westover's view O'Connor's performance "ties together the best elements of both versions" of "Be a Clown" in the earlier film.[66]

In 2018 scholar Alan Nadel tied the humiliation of the character Lina Lamont in the film to a more general "diminishment of female agency after World War II" in the US.[67] Nadel's interpretation is just a small part of an in-depth, book-length exploration of cold war social and film history. Lina's lack of depth as a character was partially redressed in Comden and Green's 1985 stage version of the film, discussed below.

Also in 2018 Lloyd Whitesell published a detailed analysis and discussion of the "Broadway Ballet," including an interpretive sectional table rewarding close study, in his lively book *Wonderful Design*.[68] Whitesell noted that the song "Broadway Rhythm" is made up of four different phrases that can be rearranged freely, including one, "Oh, that Broadway rhythm," that is open-ended, a musical version of a genuine yell.[69] He cheerfully observed that the ballet "interrupts the plot" and "doesn't advance it at all" while also acknowledging the "critical acumen" of Raymond Knapp, another scholar who connected the ballet to the film's portrayals of how sound film displaced live performance in an earlier study.[70] Refreshingly, Whitesell also pointed out that it is perfectly logical for the ballet to be "pure diversion and indulgence," in line with its clearly plotted function as "an imaginary visualization of a cinematic production number still at the idea stage."[71]

In 2020 Helen Hanson shed welcome light on the history of one of the vital "movie workers in the shadows" at MGM in an article titled "Looking for Lela Simone." Focusing in on Simone's work on Kelly's solo rain dance, Hanson praised Simone's "exacting technical supervision," leading to "perfect synchronisation" and "polished production values."[72] Hanson uncovered records of a series of sound tests for "wet taps" for use in dubbing Kelly's solo rain dance recorded by Conrad Kahn and performed by Kelly's assistant Carol Haney, qualifying the attribution by Dabholkar and Hess of the final dubs of these taps to Kelly discussed in chapter 4.[73] Hanson concluded that the number worked so well due to Simone's "careful balancing of vocal performance, dance movement, music, and sound effects."[74]

In 2021 Talya Alon traced intertextual connections between the "Broadway Ballet" and *Broadway Melody* (1929), while also comparing Cyd Charisse's performance to Marlene Dietrich's in *Die Blaue Engel* (1930). Taking off from literary critic Harold Bloom's concept of artists strongly misreading one another, Alon also looked at how two of the films within the film mocked themselves. To do so, *The Royal Rascal* used mimicry and exaggerated gestures, while *The Dueling Cavalier* employed "sound intensified out of proportion."[75] While scholars continue to have their say about *Singin'*, artists in various fields have also referenced the film in takeoffs, remixes, and original works. Surprisingly, for a work considered by many critics to be so cinematic, one of these remakes is a stage show, authored by the same durable duo who created the story in the first place.

"Why Bother?"—*Singin'*, the Stage Show

On June 30, 1983, *Singin' in the Rain,* also written by Comden and Green (now aged sixty-six and sixty-nine, respectively), opened at the Palladium in London's West End theater district. Cosmo danced to Cole Porter's "Be a Clown" instead of "Make 'Em Laugh," and the Gershwins' song "Fascinatin' Rhythm" was interpolated into the show. The production was directed by former 1950s rock and roll performer Tommy Steele, who also starred in the show as Don Lockwood. The production was panned by Robert Cushman in the *Observer* as "too slow." He went further, asking "Why bother? Why try to reproduce—not reinterpret—a masterpiece?"[76] Fans disagreed; the show ran for more than two years, closing on September 28, 1985. It was then revived in London in June 1989.[77]

On July 2, 1985, a new production with a revised book by Comden and Green opened on Broadway, closing on May 18, 1986, after thirty-eight previews and 367 performances.[78] The dance critic for the *New York Times* published a sympathetic preview of the Broadway production with new direction and choreography by Twyla Tharp.[79] But when the show finally opened (after two postponements during previews) theater critic Frank Rich panned the result, writing "Tharp has failed to meet—indeed, even to consider—the central challenge of transposing a quintessentially cinematic work to the theater."[80] The paper did publish an opposing appreciation from an audience member in the letters column. "It was fun and light, there was humor, the sets were fantastic, and the dancing and voices were splendid," wrote Jack Barchas, who had traveled from California to see the show.[81]

It was theatergoers like Barchas who saved the day. As Samuel Freedman reported in the *Times* two months later, "*Variety* tallied 12 unfavorable reviews, five mixed ones and but four positive nods: for most shows, an obituary."[82] But the producers kept the show open, and despite the reviews people kept coming. By early September the show was selling "above its $250,000 break-even point each week."[83] According to an industry survey "the musical drew only 10 percent of its audience from Manhattan, but it got 16 percent from the outer boroughs, 34 percent from the suburbs, 31 percent from the rest of the United States and 10 percent from overseas. Sixty percent of the audience was older than 35."[84] Forty percent of the audience, in other words, was made up of tourists visiting the city. Clearly *Singin'* had acquired a worldwide reputation as a worthwhile entertainment by the 1980s.

One of the highlights of the full-length rental version of the show is an added number for Lina, a plaintive lament, "What's Wrong with Me?" with lyrics by Earl Brent and Edward Heyman and music by Nacio Brown. It first appeared in *The Kissing Bandit* (1948), sung by Katherine Grayson, then by Frank Sinatra as each gazed, alone, into a mirror and regretted not having kissed the other during a previous encounter.[85] After being consoled by her pal Zelda, Lina sings to her own reflection in her dressing room, airing her grief at Don's rejection of her affections. Giving Lina a chance to sing her side of the story is a brilliant stroke.

A new production opened in London at the National Theatre on June 22, 2000, directed by Jude Kelly, employing three video screens and computer graphics as set elements, with new choreography by Stephen Mear.[86] Another new production, directed by Paul Kerryson and starring ballet dancer Adam Cooper as Don, opened to mixed reviews at the Sadler's Wells Theatre in 2004 and yet was revived twice, at the Palace Theatre in 2012 (to better reviews) and back at the Sadler's Wells in 2020.[87] The show enjoyed a production in Paris, again with choreography by Mear, directed by Robert Carsen, presented in two brief runs at the Théâtre du Châtelet (a venue with 2,500 seats) in 2015 and 2016.[88] Taking arms against a sea of fans, in a review in the *New York Times* international edition Roslyn Sulcas maintained that nothing in the stage version came close to matching the film's "transcendent visions of joy."[89]

In 1998 Comden and Green, too, said they had been reluctant to adapt *Singin' in the Rain* for the stage. "We fought bitterly the idea of turning 'Singin' in the Rain' into a Broadway show. It was a movie, not a staged [*sic*] production. But we had no say in the matter or money. Neither did the director."[90] Despite critics who panned the stage show as a pale imitation of the film and the ambivalence of its writers, *Singin'* now has a life in the theater as well as on the screen.

References, Takeoffs, and Remixes

O'Connor performed perhaps the first homage to *Singin'* onscreen when he was reunited with Reynolds in the follow-up MGM musical *I Love Melvin* (1953), directed by Don Weis. The pair sing a duet "We Have Never Met as Yet" (written for the film, with lyrics by Mack Gordon and music by Josef Myrow) set in Central Park in the morning. As the two young people at the

Figure 5.2 Donald O'Connor perched on a lamp post in *I Love Melvin* (1953).

center of the story walk to work separately, O'Connor leaps up on a lamppost and assumes Kelly's signature stance[91] (at 11:52; see figure 5.2).

Stanley Kubrick's 1971 "brilliant but disappointing" R-rated film adaptation of Anthony Burgess's 1962 novel *A Clockwork Orange* wrenched the title song into shocking new dramaturgical terrain.[92] The protagonist, Alex DeLarge (played by Malcolm McDowell), sings the title song a cappella while he and his gang assault a wealthy couple within the first few minutes of the film. After undergoing aversion therapy, Alex sings the song again while bathing, joyfully, remembering nothing of his previous actions. In Kubrick's final twist on the song's associations as a shared icon of carefree joy, Gene Kelly's easeful performance of the song from the soundtrack of the 1952 film plays under the closing credits, powerfully evoking a sunny state of mind at exactly the wrong moment for a somber, shocked audience still taking it all in. These juxtapositions create shocking dissonances between music and action that transgress audience's expectations around how sounds and images in film usually work together.[93]

A Clockwork Orange reinterprets other musical works as well, including pieces by Mozart and Beethoven. But Kubrick's use of "Singin' in the Rain" as a recurring refrain, in a film so far from the conventional musical genre, is especially grim and memorable. In 1991 Michael Jackson also mixed references to Kelly's dancing with outbursts of violence in a lengthy music video, discussed below.

Hoping to profit from nostalgia for the studio era and the continuing popularity of *Singin' in the Rain* and *The Wizard of Oz*, both television perennials by this time, MGM repackaged musical numbers from its back catalogue into a series of family-friendly, G-rated anthologies. Kelly, Donen, Reynolds, and O'Connor participated as narrators in three celebratory collections titled *That's Entertainment* (1974, 1976 [*II*], and 1994 [*III*]), and *That's Dancing!* (1985). In a very positive review of the 1974 release, *New York Times* critic Nora Sayre wrote that the excerpts "run long enough so that you can re-experience the original. Hence this isn't nostalgia, it's history."[94] All four of these retrospectives included excerpts from *Singin' in the Rain*. Even Kathy's cut number "You Are My Lucky Star" reappeared, included in the 1994 anthology.

Reducing *Singin' in the Rain* and other MGM musicals into smaller intercut fragments was a strategy pursued in *That's Dancing* (1985), a chronological history of dance narrated mostly by Kelly ending with excerpts from "Beat It," a music video starring Michael Jackson. A similar aesthetic emphasizing rapid montages came to dominate the "MTV: Music Television" cable channel introduced in 1981.[95] Rick James and many other popular African American performers were repeatedly passed over by MTV's programmers until the huge sales of Jackson's *Thriller* (1983) made the network's position commercially untenable.[96]

John Landis's eleven-minute film featuring "Black or White," Michael Jackson's first single from the album *Dangerous* (1991), begins with scenes of comic violence featuring a child star of the era, Macaulay Culkin. According to *Rolling Stone* "an estimated half a billion people saw the premiere" on various television networks around the world.[97] Next a complex music video incorporates medleys of dancers superimposed via green screen into dramatic settings from around the world. After the song ends, within a quasi-documentary shot of a crowded indoor soundstage recalling similar self-reflexive moments in *Singin'*, a black panther appears.[98] The panther exits, then digitally metamorphoses into a human: Jackson. The singer dons a fedora and prowls, dancing and freezing periodically in an aestheticized impression of a big cat.[99] The setting is a deserted night street modeled loosely after the set for Kelly's solo rain dance, equipped with a similar streetlamp

Figure 5.3 Michael Jackson next to a streetlamp in "Black or White" (1991).

(see figure 5.3) Although the street is dry, quick closeups of Jackson's feet splashing down into puddles in slow motion are inserted into the sequence, which is accompanied by sound effects but no music.

After demolishing a car's windows with a crowbar and dancing atop the wreck (parked next to a streetlamp), Jackson breaks a plate glass window in a storefront with a garbage can, a direct reference to the ending of Kelly and Donen's "Alter Ego" dance sequence in *Cover Girl* (1944), in which Kelly dances and struggles with a translucent doppelgänger. The street becomes wet, although rain isn't depicted. Jackson kneels in a puddle, tearing his clothes, as a neon hotel sign explodes behind him. He morphs back into a panther and lopes away, in a crane shot mimicking the point of view for Kelly's similar departure from the scene of his solo dance. After complaints, Jackson's violent outbursts were excised from the film, which was then re-broadcast repeatedly on MTV.[100]

The *New York Times* rock critic Jon Pareles called the film "a riot of derivativeness, a kind of random replay of commercial and movie images," making no specific mention of the references to Kelly's choreography.[101] But in 1995 scholar Carol Clover read these moments as an attempt, "intentionally or not," to "'un-cover' or 'de-blackface' *Singin' in the Rain*."[102] Clover prefaced this interpretation with discussions of an overriding theme of the film, "giving credit where credit is due," and ongoing controversies around appropriations of African American artistic innovations by European American dancers including Kelly and O'Connor such as a televised incident a decade earlier.[103]

During a 1985 tribute to Kelly organized by the American Film Institute, the younger tap dancer Gregory Hines joked that he had invented a step, then discovered that Kelly had "copied" it—in a film made thirty years earlier. As the television critic John O'Connor reported in the *New York Times,* "Later [in the broadcast], the veteran Nicholas Brothers, Harold and Fayard, jokingly advise[d] Mr. Hines not to 'bother about stealing Gene Kelly's stuff— he's stolen from us.' It is meant to be a light moment, but the underpinnings are serious."[104] During their careers both Kelly and Hines mastered difficult dance gestures pioneered by the Nicholas Brothers during the swing era. As mentioned before, the Nicholas Brothers even appeared together with Kelly in the first iteration of Cole Porter's song "Be a Clown" in *The Pirate* (1948). The scene in which the three danced together was removed from some (but apparently not all) prints screened in segregated theaters in the American South.[105]

A 2005 Volkswagen TV commercial muddied these contested cultural waters further by using a electronic dance remix of Kelly's vocal performance of "Singin' in the Rain" for yet another version of the rain dance, depicting a digitized simulation of Kelly, still in suit and tie, as a break dancer. The faux Kelly swings upside down on a lamppost and turns cartwheels before stopping to admire a new car, guarded by a policeman who crosses his arms in warning. The soundtrack manipulates samples of Kelly's voice and Salinger's orchestral arrangement of Brown's music, setting them over newly composed drum and bass tracks.[106] This audio remix had been previously released on a brief album, *Wait for You,* under the title "Waiting in the Rain," credited to the Manchester, UK, producer Neil Claxton (aka Mint Royale). Although the terms weren't disclosed, Volkswagen's ad agency team sought and received permission from MGM and Kelly's widow to remake Kelly's performance, setting it within a recreation of the scene's original setting and digitally superimposing images of Kelly's face, hands, and costume over those of two dancers (although only one appears at a time), in an early example of an animated "deep fake."[107]

In 2014 dance scholar Mary Fogarty put a more positive spin on issues around authenticity and appropriation in an intertextual deconstruction of both Kelly's rain dance and the Volkswagen commercial. While acknowledging the validity of Clover's criticism of *Singin'* as mute on the issue of race, Fogarty countered that "Gene Kelly acknowledged the influence of both African American dance forms and Irish dance for his style in interviews rather than the film itself" and "appreciated the hip-hop dance styles that had emerged since his time."[108] She pointed out that while not explicitly naming African American sources, "in *Singin' in the Rain*, the high and low divisions of art are often parodied."[109] For Fogarty, the break dancing featured in the Volkswagen commercial, which she identified as choreographed and performed by David "Elsewhere" Bernal and Donnie "Crumbs" Counts, were creative "remixes" rather than derivative "covers"— reinventions of the original with their own artistic integrity.[110] The source of their remixes was also clearly acknowledged.[111] Fogarty did not discuss a slightly later, related appropriation of Kelly's performance, this time on a television talent show in the UK.

In 2008 George Sampson, a working-class teenager of European descent from Northern England, won first place in a contest on *Britain's Got Talent*, break dancing to Mint Royale's remix of "Singin' in the Rain."[112] More than fourteen million people viewed his performance. Sampson unintentionally re-enacted the colorblind racism of Hollywood but from divergent class and generational subject positions.[113] Was his performance a derivative cover or an inventive remix? His audience was already familiar not only with Kelly's original dance but with the Volkswagen commercial and Mint Royale's remix. After Sampson's performance, sales of the remix, this time as a digital audio download, surged anew, pushing it to No. 1 for a week on the UK Singles Chart.[114]

A follow-up 2009 music video placed Sampson within a chorus line of dancers from divergent racial backgrounds. In an introductory vignette Sampson is turned away by a Black bouncer from a dance club because he is underage.[115] Another music video for Mint Royale's "Waiting in the Rain" was also released in 2009, featuring an unidentified Black break dancer performing in a tiled pedestrian tunnel with digitally animated figures assembled from bits of flotsam and jetsam.[116] In 2019 Sampson danced brief duets with three younger Caucasian contestants, again to the Mint Royale remix, on *Britain's Got Talent* during a retrospective about past winners.[117]

Sexuality was the subtext for another round of television remixes back in the States. For the out gay character Kurt in the second season of the long-running TV series *Glee* (2009–15) O'Connor's performance of "Make 'Em Laugh" was not only a classic but a signifier for queer identity. In a September 2010 episode Kurt described "Make 'Em Laugh" inaccurately as a duet rather than a solo to a new acquaintance who he was also quietly sounding out about sexual preference.[118] In November 2010 the makers of the series fulfilled Kurt's version of history by presenting "Make 'Em Laugh" as a male duet dance in a novel hip-hop–inspired arrangement of Freed and Brown's song. After recovering from a bout of the flu by watching his favorite feel-good movie, *Singin' in the Rain*, over and over, the school's Caucasian glee club director dances a modified version of O'Connor's steps with a male Asian American student as a partner.[119] The finale of the same episode featured a hip-hop arrangement of "Singin' in the Rain" staged in the style of Rihanna and Jay-Z's music video for the song "Umbrella" (2007). The images in "Umbrella" make oblique references to the film via dance sequences on a wet stage while digital sparks rain down and Rihanna sings "baby, it's raining."[120] These remixes of numbers and dialogue about *Singin'* in *Glee* connected engagement with film musical traditions to negotiations around sexual preference and gender identity among adolescents and emerging adults. This age group was a large part of the series' audience every week.

Singin' also becomes a shared global cultural monument in a recent music video featuring the Korean band BTS. The K-pop septet remixed several visual references to dance numbers in *Singin'* without quoting any of the music in the music video for their own original song "Boy with Luv" (2019). The group jumps over, then collapses on a couch, emulating the number "Good Morning." The group prances through a forest of lampposts, evoking Chris Burden's sculpture in downtown Los Angeles also inspired by Kelly's solo.[121] J-Hope [Jung Ho-seok] swings on one of the lampposts, Kelly-style. Suddenly the group are driving (virtually) down a brightly lit avenue (while still sitting on the bright yellow couch), joined by the American singer Halsey in a distant echo of Kelly's first ride with Reynolds down a similarly virtual avenue. The music video ends with a visual tribute to the "Broadway Ballet."[122] By the end of 2022 the video had been viewed more than 1.6 billion times. For the band's younger fans, the video may have been educational as well as enjoyable. While the message is not as pointed as in *Glee*, Korean and American performers join together to re-enact and celebrate what has become a shared point of reference. *Singin'* may no longer be just an American classic but a transnational one.

Back in the UK in 2020, a commercial rejoinder to the Volkswagen ad appeared in the form of a clothing commercial documenting an original, energetic daytime street dance performed by a multiracial quartet (Kevin Bago, Robinson Cassarino, Chantel Foo, and Zhane Samuels) clad in Burberry attire, augmented with special effects. A new hip-hop remix of the song "Singin' in the Rain" produced by Joe Murphy, Jonty Howard, and Emily Pritchard, sung by Dréya Mac, a Black female rapper and choreographer from West London provided the soundtrack.[123] After rim shots and hand claps introduce the beat, Mac enters, substituting the syllable "mmm" for "doo" in a new version of the introductory hum, outlining a bass line rocking back and forth from tonic to dominant, then echoing Eden's version of the riff as crooned by Kelly, first on "mmm," then on a new vocable, "nah." Mac sings just the opening A section of the song before returning to riffs, this time repeating the evocative phrase "ready for love." Next, she begins accompanying herself with descants (via the magic of multitracking), humming the song's historic vocable, "doo," chanting the next line of lyrics, then crafting a rising, riveting coda by combining the words "singin' in the rain" with "ready for love" in free counterpoint.

Elaborate digital special effects combined with live Steadicam work (also depicted in some online versions of the ad) simulate a storm of icy snowballs just missing the dancers as they make their way to an idyllic beach. The holiday advertisement for Burberry raincoats was photographed by Katelin Arizmendi and choreographed by a trio of dancers who at the time also headed the Ballet National de Marseille, Marine Brutti, Jonathan Debrouwer, and Arthur Harel[124] (see figure 5.4). By representing a variety of colors and genders, this remix of both dance and music gave Kelly's solo dance in the rain a refreshing intercultural spin.

Rather than bliss, the dancers in "Pushing Boundaries" operate within an atmosphere full of palpable risks: digital chunks of snow and ice, ranging in size from baseballs to haybale-size blocks, which the dancers use as steppingstones to leap onto a tall garbage dumpster at one point. An office worker in a black suit scurries across the screen, cowering under his briefcase; but the dancers continue casually sauntering down the street, dodging icy missiles from the sky as if there were nothing to it. They not only dance toward the moving camera in the best Kelly/Donen manner but also address the camera directly, staring at us through the lens.

Figure 5.4 Dancers (*left to right*) Robinson Cassarino, Chantel Foo, Kevin Bago, and Zhane Samuels in "Pushing Boundaries" (2020).

Suddenly the gigantic hailstones freeze in mid-air (1:15). The dancers, working together, shoot a bolt of kinetic energy up into the sky, demolishing ice balls all along the way. The two male dancers partner one another, lifting and spinning their bodies. At the end of the street, a beach appears (1:25). The dancers rush toward the sea, and one rips off his Burberry clothing and dives right in, as digital snowballs fall harmlessly all around him. The moment brings an analogous beach scene in *Daughters of the Dust* (1991) to mind, at 45:10 in that unforgettable independent film directed by Julie Dash.

Conclusions: Whither *Singin'*?

The short list surveyed here of films, stage and television shows, music videos, and commercials referring to *Singin' in the Rain* were chosen because of their aesthetic approach, their popularity, or the issues they raised, particularly around race, gender, and class. Remixes of songs from the film have drawn on contemporary African American styles, just as Kelly, O'Connor, and "Skip" Martin did in their day. This process has helped to bring the original film's unpaid debts to Black culture closer to the surface. Queer readings of the film have crept into popular television series aimed at tweens and teens like *Glee*. Kelly's determination to inject a working-class sensibility into

Hollywood choreography has been embraced and extended by dancers of all colors in the UK and France who also love hip-hop. As this book goes to press writer/director Damien Chazelle's feature film *Babylon* and Daveed Diggs's performance of the song "Singing in the Rain" in a ruined, flooded synagogue in a recent episode of the streaming series Extrapolations are among the latest examples of the new directions artistic engagement with *Singin'* can lead to, now and in the future.[125]

Along with wisecracks and slapstick Comden and Green served up studies of foppish celebrities and frenzied fans, the hierarchies and injustices of the studio system, and engrossing dramatizations of filmmaking processes. As further developed in the stage show, there is a tragic dimension to the story's intensely likable villain Lina Lamont, so ambitious, so shallow, so beautiful, so unintentionally funny, and so emblematic of the era's gender inequalities. The 1920s are portrayed as an era of rapid social and technological changes and new artistic frontiers. Looking backward from the cold war era of the 1950s, the film nostalgically celebrated and commemorated an era of greater creativity and freedom in American popular culture.

The final cut of *Singin'* conveys a taut sense of wholeness, despite the intertextual trunk full of old songs the creative team had to fit together like pieces left over from a dozen different jigsaw puzzles. This sense of wholeness, achieved via the multiple means (story, production, choreography, cinematography, and music) explored in earlier chapters, defies analysis to an extent. In 2002, fifty years after the film's release, an interviewer asked Cyd Charisse why she thought *Singin' in the Rain* had "endured so well." She answered, diplomatically: "I can't explain it exactly. It appeals to everybody. It has all the charm of that era [the 1920s] but does it so tongue-in-cheek and so fun."[126] Like Charisse, in 1975 Canby had pulled back from any analysis of the work. "As so often happens with something unique," he wrote, "it's rather easier to describe what it isn't than what it is. . . . 'Singin' in the Rain' is an original and I'm as hesitant to attempt to analyze it as I would be to take a clock apart."[127]

The film can indeed be read as episodic, composed of a string of numbers linked up by skit-like gags and incidents. This was the view of early reviewers including Crowther and Guernsey. But as surveyed in earlier chapters, Comden and Green created a suitable, coherent narrative; then Kelly, Donen, and Hayton interlocked story and song, creating smooth segues into and out of each number, a bit like clockwork, in fact—to assemble a marvelous musical film machine.

In 2017 scholar Hannah Lewis described Mamoulian's *Love Me Tonight* (the subject of Geoffrey Block's study in this series) as poised between "integration and cinematic stylization."[128] While making *Singin'* Kelly and Donen sought aesthetic goals similar to Mamoulian's in the earlier film: a specifically cinematic degree of "unity" achieved in part by collaborations among creators.[129] To continue to employ Lewis's analysis of integration as a starting point, at various points *Singin'* "sounds the way the costumes look," achieving an unspoken degree of "a single aesthetic unity."[130] At other moments the writers and directors merely ensured that numbers were "diegetically justified, as is typically the case in backstage musicals," while occasionally self-reflexively "highlight[ing], rather than hid[ing], cinematic techniques." [131] As a hugely popular, critically esteemed work seemingly made whole via Kelly's authorial approach to cinematic choreography, *Singin'*, like *Love Me Tonight* before it, has offered abundant inspiration to future performers, dancemakers, and filmmakers.

Meanwhile, *Singin' in the Rain* continues to make people of all ages just feel good, combining a streamlined storyline with vivid characters, memorable wisecracks and comedy, a modicum of safe romance, riveting dancing, an engaging score, sturdy songs, gorgeous sets, vintage props, awesome costumes, and virtuosic camera work. This simple, safe-for-children modern fairy tale is not simplistic. It is not just the combination comedy, musical, and history lesson Basinger described but a social satire with a point of view on human nature and morality—what Comden called "a deep thread of real feeling."[132]

Notes

Series Editor's Foreword

1. Wendy Wasserstein, "Holiday Movies: After 50 Years, It's Still a Glorious Feeling," *New York Times*, November 3, 2002, A2.

Preface

1. Pauline Kael, *I Lost It at the Movies* (Boston: Little, Brown, 1965), 142.
2. Basinger, *The Movie Musical!* 439.
3. Ibid.
4. Ibid., 440.
5. Ibid., 444.
6. Betty Comden, quoted in Baer, *Classic American Films*, 9.
7. Chabrol, "Que Ma Joie Demeure," 55.
8. Eugene Archer, "Museum to Show Gene Kelly Films: 9 of Dancer's Movies Listed—Reception to Honor Him," *New York Times*, August 10, 1962, 11.
9. Kevin Thomas, "Gene Kelly Singing the Blues Over State of U.S. Musicals," *Los Angeles Times*, August 30, 1966, C16.
10. Behlmer groups *Excess Baggage* with a genre of musicals depicting "the trials and tribulations of a married vaudeville team," along with *Mother Wore Tights* (1947) and *You're My Everything* (1949). Behlmer, *America's Favorite Movies*, 253–54.
11. Betty Comden, quoted in "Theater Talk: Remembering Betty Comden."
12. On the other hand, all those Oscars went to creators behind the camera; none of the performers in *An American in Paris* were nominated; see "The 24th Academy Awards, 1952," Academy of Motion Picture Arts and Sciences, https://www.oscars.org/oscars/ceremonies/1952.
13. "Singin' in the Rain," Google Ngram Viewer, accessed August 4, 2021, https://books.google.com/ngrams/graph?content=Singin+%27+in+the+Rain&year_start=1800&year_end=2019&corpus=26&smoothing=3&direct_url=t1%3B%2CSingin%20%27%20in%20the%20Rain%3B%2Cc0#t1%3B%2CSingin%20'%20in%20the%20Rain%3B%2Cc0

Chapter 1: Creating "a Movie about the Movies"

1. Betsy Blair, *The Memory of All That*, 143.
2. Hugh Fordin, typed, corrected transcript of an interview with Gene Kelly, "Research for 'The World of Entertainment!'," 1950–59, Arthur Freed Papers, Box 22, Folder 14, USC.
3. Comden and Green, "Foreword," *Singin' in the Rain* (1972), 2.
4. Bingen et al., *MGM: Hollywood's Greatest Backlot*, Foreword by Debbie Reynolds, 8.
5. Denfeld, "Future Hollywood Producer Arthur Freed."
6. Comden and Green, "Foreword," *Singin' in the Rain* (1972), 1.
7. "Olden Days in Hollywood" is a line from Betty Comden et al., Revuers radio script, April 30, 1940, *Fun with The Revuers*, Comden and Green Papers, Series I: Scripts (1933–1979), Billy Rose Theatre Collection, NYPL, 14.
8. Eyman, *The Lion of Hollywood*, 1.
9. Ibid.
10. Ibid., 1–2.
11. Ibid., 1. See also photo of gate in Bingen et al., *MGM: Hollywood's Greatest Backlot*, 26.
12. Actor Ann Rutherford, quoted in Walter Wagner, *You Must Remember This* (New York: G. P. Putnam's Sons, 1975), 204; quoted also in Eyman, *The Lion in Hollywood*, 1.
13. Eyman, *The Lion in Hollywood*, 2.
14. See "Loew's, Inc." *Fortune* (August 1939): 25–30+; reprinted in Tino Balio, ed., *The American Film Industry*, rev. ed. (Madison: University of Wisconsin Press, 1985 [1976]), 334–50.

15. MGM, United Artists, Columbia, and Universal Studios were the "et al." companies. *United States v. Paramount Pictures, Inc., et al.* 334 U.S. 131 (1948). Accessed online on August 14, 2022, at: https://tile.loc.gov/storage-services/service/ll/usrep/usrep334/usrep334131/usrep334131.pdf.
16. Doherty, *Hollywood's Censor*, 292.
17. Ibid., 228.
18. Jason Mittell, "The 'Classic Network System' in the US (Genre Cycles: Innovation, Imitation, Saturation)," in *The Television History Book*, ed. Michele Hilmes (London: British Film Institute, 2003), 44.
19. Herbert Kupferberg, "The World's Biggest Movie Studio Dazzles a Tourist," *New York Herald Tribune*, April 6, 1952, D1. See also US Bureau of Labor Statistics, "CPI Inflation Calculator." Figures are approximate.
20. In addition to Mayer, these were Eddie Mannix, Harry Rapf, and Benny Thau. Schatz, *The Genius of the System*, 442.
21. Ibid., 447.
22. See profit figures for 1946 for the major studios, ibid., 441.
23. "Daily Progress Reports and Picture Estimate." Budget memo signed by Walter C. Strohm, June 18, 1951, Production Manager, Arthur Freed Papers, Box 23, Folder 3, USC.
24. Ibid.
25. Ibid.
26. Ibid.
27. "Income of Persons Up 10 Percent in 1951 (Advance data, April 1952 sample survey)," United States Census Bureau, Report Number P60-10, September 26, 1952, https://www.census.gov/library/publications/1952/demo/p60-010.html.
28. Knox, *The Magic Factory*, 17–18.
29. Letter from Irving Lazar to Betty Comden, March 14, 1951, Business Correspondence, Comden and Green Papers, Box 18, Folder 12, NYPL.
30. "Daily Progress Reports and Picture Estimate."
31. See the quote from O'Connor in chapter 4 from "Ebertfest Flashback: Donald O'Connor on 'Singin' in the Rain'" [interview transcript] (website post, April 27, 2003), accessed October 24, 2022, https://www.rogerebert.com/festivals/ebertfest-flashback-donald-oconnor-on-singin-in-the-rain.
32. "Daily Progress Reports and Picture Estimate."
33. Helen Gould, "Millard Mitchell Still Fights Not To Be a Star," *New York Herald Tribune*, August 24, 1952, D3.
34. "Millard Mitchell, Actor, Dead at 50," *New York Times*, October 14, 1953, 29.
35. "Daily Progress Reports and Picture Estimate."
36. Ibid.
37. Ibid.
38. Ibid.
39. Ibid.; see also Philip Scheuer, "Rita Moreno's Principal Aim Is to be Bullfighter," *Los Angeles Times*, October 26, 1952, E1.
40. "Daily Progress Reports and Picture Estimate."
41. Fordin, "Research for 'The World of Entertainment!'," 1950–59, Arthur Freed Papers, Box 22, Folder 14, USC.
42. "Movieland Briefs," *Los Angeles Times*, May 10, 1948, 17.
43. "Excess Baggage," AFI Catalog of Feature Films. See also Andrew Buchman, "Developing the Screenplay for *Singin' in the Rain* (1952)," in Broomfield-McHugh, ed., *The Oxford Handbook of the Hollywood Musical*, 315–16. Jack McGowan, who wrote *Excess Baggage*, also wrote MGM's *Broadway Melody of 1938* and co-wrote *Babes in Arms* (1939) among other projects.
44. "Excess Baggage," *Wikipedia*, This poster is in the public domain in the United States. Accessed October 21, 2022. Source: Employee(s) of MGM—http://www.doctormacro.com/Movie%20Summaries/E/Excess%20Baggage%20%281928%29.htm.
45. Jack MacGowan, "'Excess Baggage,' a play in three acts." Typescript, n.d. [1927?]. American Play Company Records, Box 33, Folder 1, NYPL.
46. *Cover Girl* (1944), a tremendously successful film, employs a similar plot: a female partner more successful than a male one.
47. Ben Feiner Jr., "Original Singing in the Rain-Cp [Cp?] rough draft of story outline from Ben Feiner, Jr.," January 25 and 28, 1949, Turner/MGM Scripts, Folder 2642-f.S-1233, AL.
48. Ibid., 4.

49. 6/18/51 Budget memo, signed by Walter C. Strohm, Production Manager. Daily Progress Reports and Picture Estimate (budget), Arthur Freed Papers, Box 22, Folder 13, AL. I erroneously transposed Davis's payroll records ahead a year, to 1951, in a table in my chapter on *Singin'* in *The Oxford Handbook of Hollywood Musicals,* ed. Dominic Broomfield-McHugh, 311.

50. Comden and Green, "Foreword," *Singin' in the Rain* (1972), 4.

51. Budget memo signed by Walter C. Strohm, June 18, 1951, Production Manager, Arthur Freed Papers, Box 23, Folder 3, USC. Comden and Green were paid for twenty-one unbroken weeks of work between May 29 and October 21, 1950, and they dated their "strike" as beginning the week after they arrived in Hollywood, after a long meeting with Freed. Under their contract with MGM, they also had a financial incentive for taking this stance. If they wrote all the lyrics for a film, they each got an additional $25,000, plus royalties.

52. Comden and Green, "Foreword," *Singin' in the Rain* (1972), 4.

53. Betty Comden et al., Revuers radio script, April 30, 1940, *Fun with The Revuers,* Comden and Green Papers, Series I: Scripts (1933–1979), NYPL, 14 and 19.

54. Baer, *Classic American Films,* 5–6.

55. Ibid., 3; and "Singin' in the Rain," 1950-08-10 MGM script 2642-f.1234 (dated August 10–September 14, 1950), Turner/MGM Scripts, AL, 51 and 58–59. The villain's line in both the first and second drafts is "heh, heh, heh" rather than "yes, yes, yes." See also the "OK" duplicated draft script with pages of duplicated typed dated revisions inserted (dated April 11–July 20, 1951), Adolph Green Papers, Box 12, Folder 3, NYPL, 63.

56. Gene Kelly, quoted in Curtis Lee Hanson, "An Interview with Gene Kelly," *Cinema* 3, no. 4 (December 1966): 26.

57. Comden and Green, "Foreword," *Singin' in the Rain* (1972), 7–8.

58. Comden and Green, "Singin' in the Rain," Temporary Complete Script (with revisions to October 14, 1950), Comden and Green Papers, Box 9, Folder 6, NYPL, 80 and 91.

59. *Singin' in the Rain* script (with revisions to October 14, 1950), Comden & Green Papers, Box 9, Folder 6, NYPL, 44.

60. Caleb Taylor Boyd, *Oscar Levant: Pianist, Gershwinite, Middlebrow Media Star* (PhD diss., Washington University in St. Louis, 2020), xv.

61. Comden and Green, "Singin' in the Rain," 1950-10-14 Temporary Complete Script, Comden and Green Papers, Box 9, Folder 6, NYPL, 60.

62. This poster is in the public domain in the United States. Source: *"Lovey Mary"* (*International Movie Database,* n.d.), accessed online on October 22, 2022 at: https://www.imdb.com/title/tt0017088/mediaviewer/rm3669100544.

63. Donald Knox, *The Magic Factory: How MGM Made "An American in Paris"* (New York: Praeger, 1973), xv.

64. Comden and Green, "'Singin' in the Rain' composite script #33," October 14, 1950, with some revisions through October 20, Turner/MGM Scripts, Folder S.1237, AL, 91. A portion of this ending (pages 87–88) is posted online at the Academy Library's website, accessed December 18, 2022, at https://www.oscars.org/collection-highlights/singin-rain/?fid=41961.

65. Comden and Green, "'Singin' in the Rain' Temporary Complete Script, Comden and Green Papers, Box 9, Folder 6, NYPL, October 14 1950, 2–3.

66. Ibid., 3.

67. Comden and Green, "Singin' in the Rain," April 11, 1951, with revisions inserted dated as late as July 20, 1951, Betty Comden Papers, Box 12, Folder 11, NYPL, 3. This second draft of the screenplay was known as the "OK" script since Freed approved it for use during production.

68. Ibid., 23; and Comden and Green, "'Singin' in the Rain' Temporary Incomplete" script, August 10, 1950, with inserted pages dated as late as September 14, Turner/MGM Scripts, Folder 2642-f.1234, AL, 16.

69. This part of the scene was also revised between the first and "OK" screenplays and then altered further during production.

70. Comden and Green, "'Singin' in the Rain' Temporary Incomplete" script, August 10, 1950, with inserted pages dated as late as September 14), Turner/MGM Scripts, Folder 2642-f.1234, AL, 17.

71. Ibid., 70.

72. Ibid., 88.

73. Ibid., 6.

74. Comden and Green, "Singin' in the Rain," April 11, 1951, with revisions inserted dated as late as July 20, 1951, Betty Comden Papers, Box 12, Folder 11, NYPL, 86.

75. Comden and Green, "'Singin' in the Rain' Temporary Incomplete" script, August 10, 1950, with inserted pages dated as late as September 14, Turner/MGM Scripts, Folder 2642-f.1234, AL, 78.
76. The writers pursued a similar strategy for the principal romance in their next screenplay, for *The Band Wagon* (1953).
77. Comden and Green, "Singin' in the Rain Temporary Incomplete" script, August 10, 1950, with inserted pages dated as late as September 14, Turner/MGM Scripts, Folder 2642-f.1234, AL, 46.
78. For discussions of Jolson and race in *Singin'* and a related homage in a music video starring Michael Jackson, "Black or White," see Clover, "Dancin' in the Rain," 722–47, discussed in chapter 5.
79. Comden and Green, "Singin' in the Rain," Temporary Complete Script, October 14, 1950, Comden and Green Papers, Box 9, Folder 6, NYPL, 41.
80. Comden and Green, "Singin' in the Rain," April 11, 1951, with revisions inserted dated as late as July 20, 1951, Betty Comden Papers, Box 12, Folder 11, NYPL, 42.
81. Carol Oja also points out "the blueprint it [*On the Town*] provided for the much more famous *Singin' in the Rain*." Carol J. Oja, *Bernstein Meets Broadway: Collaborative Art in a Time of War* (New York: Oxford University Press, 2014), 114.
82. Comden and Green, *Singin' in the Rain: Story and Screenplay*, 1.
83. *An Evening with Gene Kelly*, interview with Gavin Millar (BBC, 1974), 24:50 and 24:35 .
84. Silverman, *Dancing on the Ceiling*, 149.
85. Ibid.
86. Stanley Donen, quoted in Joseph Andrew Casper, *Stanley Donen* (Metuchen, NJ: Scarecrow Press, 1983), 44.
87. Comden and Green, "Foreword," *Singin' in the Rain*, 6.
88. Ibid.; Kevin Brownlow and John Kobal, "The Rise and Fall of John Gilbert," in *Hollywood: The Pioneers* (New York: Knopf, 1979), 192–203; MGM script 2642-f.1234 1950.08.10-09.14, 57.
89. Brownlow and Kobal, 193.
90. Jill Nelmes and Jule Selbo, eds., *Women Screenwriters: An International Guide* (Houndmills, Basingstoke, Hampshire: Palgrave Macmillan, 2015), between 726 and 859 [page pending].
91. Betty Comden, Postmarked, two-page letter to self, sent by registered mail, receipt requested, March 24, 1981, Betty Comden Papers, Box 11 Folder 2, NYPL.
92. Ibid.
93. Ibid.
94. Ethel Barrymore accepted the award for Holliday at the ceremony, after the melody for Freed and Brown's song "You Are My Lucky Star" was played by the house orchestra. See "Academy Awards Acceptance Speech Database," Academy of Motion Pictures Arts and Sciences, n.d., online at: http://aaspeechesdb.oscars.org/link/023-3/.
95. Kelly claimed that Hagen had been Holliday's understudy in the role, but she isn't listed as such in the *Internet Broadway Database*; see Hirschhorn, *Gene Kelly: A Biography* (New York: St. Martin's, 1984 [1974]), 181; and "Jean Hagen," *Internet Broadway Database*, accessed online on June 27, 2022, at: https://www.ibdb.com/broadway-cast-staff/jean-hagen-97242.
96. Dabholkar and Hess, *"Singin' in the Rain,"* 67.
97. Arthur Freed interviewed in Arthur Kobal, *People Will Talk* (New York: Alfred A. Knopf, 1985), 651. Murray, like Haines, was blacklisted by Louis B. Mayer after refusing assignments at MGM. Her few sound film appearances were unsuccessful. See Michael Ankerich, *Mae Murray: The Girl with the Bee-Stung Lips* (Lexington: University Press of Kentucky, 2013), 214.
98. See Jane Feuer, "The Self-Reflexive Musical," 444–51.
99. Feuer, *The Hollywood Musical*, 102 and 107.

Chapter 2: Revising the Screenplay

1. "Singin' in the Rain 1951" including screenplay sections and dialogue by Joseph Fields, 2643.f-S-1241 (July 26, 1951, and August 7, 1951), Turner/MGM Scripts, AL. Fields, the son of vaudeville legend Lew Fields, co-wrote the scripts for both the stage and film versions of *Gentlemen Prefer Blondes* (1949, 1952) with Anita Loos. On Broadway he collaborated with Joseph Chodorov to write many shows, including *Wonderful Town* (1953), and worked with Oscar Hammerstein II to adapt C. Y. Lee's novel *The Flower Drum Song* (1957) into a 1958 Broadway show.
2. This phrase is not in the first draft; it was added to the second "OK" draft in 1951. See Comden and Green, "Singin' in the Rain," dated April 11, 1951, with revisions inserted dated as late as July 20, 1951, Betty Comden Papers, Box 12, Folder 11, NYPL, 4. This second draft of the screenplay was known as the "OK" script since Freed approved it for use during production.

3. The first violin part bears some resemblance to the opening phrase of Edward "Duke" Ellington's composition "In a Sentimental Mood" (1935), as does Salinger's underscoring for Don's cut solo version of "All I Do Is Dream of You," discussed in chapter 3.

4. *Cover Girl* includes the "Alter-Ego Dance," composed of a series of composited shots. Accessed December 7, 2022, https://www.youtube.com/watch?v = v4_77c52xBc. Donen made only one more film as co-director with Kelly, *It's Always Fair Weather* (1955).

5. Robert Welkos, "Obituaries; Donald O'Connor, 78; Entertainer Immortalized by 'Singin' in the Rain.'" *Los Angeles Times,* September 28, 2003, B22. See also Mindy Aloff, filmography in "Remembering a Hoofer: An Interview [in 1979] with Donald O'Connor," *DanceView Times,* New York Edition, October 7, 2003, accessed online on June 8, 2024 at: https://danceviewtimes.com/dvny/features/2003/o'connor.html.

6. McGilligan, *Backstory 2* (1991), 81.

7. "Singin' in the Rain / (Dialogue Cutting Continuity) / (Film Editor ... Adrienne Fazan, A.C.E.)," Continuity Script prepared for film editing (both archival copies dated March 17, 1952; exact date unknown), CTR 1390 (this copy includes all music cues), NYPL; and Betty Comden Papers, Box 12, folder 12, NYPL. The continuity script is unpaged but divided into reels; all stage directions from Comden and Green's drafts are omitted. Release prints of feature films were routinely divided into 22-minute-long reels of film that were played one after the other, alternating between two projectors. The projectionist had to execute these transitions carefully to make them as seamless as possible. For a description of the projectionist's work see James Barron, "Projectionists Are Keeping the Dying Art of Celluloid Alive," *New York Times,* April 14, 2019, A18.

8. Panel Discussion, "Singin' in the Rain 50th Anniversary," at 14:42, accessed December 10, 2022, https://www.youtube.com/watch?v = F0JYyT-acGk.

9. Stanley Donen, quoted in Silverman, *Dancing on the Ceiling,* 338.

10. Dabholkar and Hess, *Singin' in the Rain,* 188; Behlmer, *America's Favorite Movies,* 268; Fordin, *MGM's Greatest Musicals,* 362; Silverman, *Dancing on the Ceiling,* 155; and "What a Glorious Feeling" all cite Fordin's figures.

11. Fordin, *MGM's Greatest Musicals,* 359.

12. Ibid., 362. Fordin himself qualified his estimates, stating that " 'box office gross' is used whimsically in movie industry accounting," but also asserted that his numbers were "actually the net return to the studio for the given production." See *MGM's Greatest Musicals,* viii n1. See also Joel Finler, *The Hollywood Story* (London: Wallflower Press, 2003 [1988]), 41–50; and John Izod, *Hollywood and the Box Office, 1895–1986* (New York: Columbia University Press, 1988), 132–50.

13. Arthur Freed, quoted in Edwin Schallert, "Musicals Look to Rich Future: Even Film Grand Opera's in Range, Insists Producer of Smash Series," *Los Angeles Times,* April 15, 1951, D1.

14. See "Sunset Blvd.," AFI Catalog of Feature Films online, accessed March 30, 2023, at: https://catalog.afi.com/Film/26513-SUNSET-BLVD.

15. 1950-08-10 MGM script 2642-f.1234 1950.08.10-09.14, Turner/MGM Scripts, AL, 22; and at 17:37 in the finished film.

16. O'Connor may have improvised this version. The line as submitted to the censors on June 1, 1951, was "And you could charm the critics but you won't have to eat." "Motion Picture Association of America, Production Code Administration records," Margaret Herrick Library Digital Collections online.

17. Letter from Irving Lazar to Betty Comden, March 14, 1951, Business Correspondence, Comden and Green Papers, Box 18, Folder 12, NYPL.

18. Ibid.

19. Ibid.

20. Blair, *The Memory of All That,* 114–15.

21. Comden and Green, *Singin' in the Rain* (1972), 9–10.

22. Stanley Donen in "Stanley Donen Interviewed by Stephen Harvey," *Film Comment* 9, no. 4 (July–August 1973), 5.

23. Stanley Donen, quoted in Casper, *Stanley Donen,* 44. Dabholkar and Hess also marshal evidence supporting Donen's view; see their *Singin' in the Rain,* 64–65.

24. Betty Comden and Adolph Green, prefatory note, *Singin' in the Rain* (1972), ix.

25. Composite script, Comden and Green Papers, Box 9, Folder 7, NYPL. Possibly compiled in 1970 or 1971 for the script as published in 1972.

26. Donen's deposit of papers at AL covers only the years 1960–1989. "Stanley Donen Papers," Special Collections, AL. See finding aid at: https://oac.cdlib.org/findaid/ark:/13030/c8m32xdf/entire_text/.

27. From News Services, "Son Rescues Gene Kelly from Burning House," *Washington Post*, December 23, 1983, D2.

28. See Kelly's annotated script to the 1956 film *The Happy Road*, Gene Kelly Collection, Box 1, Folder 4, BU. Folder 1 in the same box (his script for *Singin' in the Rain*), although still listed in the Collection's finding aid for many years, was returned to Kelly and subsequently lost in a house fire. See finding aid online at: http://archives.bu.edu/finding-aid/finding_aid_325 881.pdf

29. "Singin' in the Rain," AFI Catalog of Feature Films online, accessed March 13, 2024, at: https://catalog.afi.com/Catalog/moviedetails/50652. IMDb also credits Jack Aldworth. "Singin' in the Rain," IMDb.com, accessed March 13, 2024: https://www.imdb.com/title/tt0045152/full credits/.

30. See "Intro to 'Make 'Em Laugh,'" typescript "From: Roger Edens," Freed Papers, Box 23, Folder 1, USC.

31. "Singin' in the Rain," 1950-10-14 Temporary Complete Script, Comden and Green Papers, Box 9, Folder 6, NYPL, 44.

32. See memo from Edens, Arthur Freed Papers, Box 23, Folder 1, USC; Fordin, *MGM's Greatest Musicals*, 359; and "Motion Picture Association of America, Production Code Administration records," Margaret Herrick Library Digital Collections online.

33. Behlmer, "America's Favorite Movies—research (SINGIN' IN THE RAIN)," Rudy Behlmer Papers, Folder 47, AL.

34. "What a Glorious Feeling," 18:07.

35. *An Evening with Gene Kelly*, 2:24. Dabholkar and Hess also argue that the bullying the three Kelly boys faced while walking to dance classes, beginning when Gene was seven years old, shaped Gene's attitudes as an adult toward dance and gender. Dabholkar and Hess, *Gene Kelly*, 8–9 and 19.

36. Delamater, *Dance in the Hollywood Musical*, 82: Clover, "Dancin' in the Rain," 728n17; Knight, *Disintegrating the Musical*, 25, 30, 247. See also "'Stealing Steps' and Signature Moves: Alternative System of Copyright" in Kraut, *Choreographing Copyright*, 127–64; and Gottschild, *Digging the Africanist Presence in American Performance*, 33–34. Clover also cites Bill "Bojangles" Robinson, John Bubbles, the Berry Brothers, and Clayton "Peg Leg" Bates as possible influences on both Kelly and O'Connor.

37. Kelly called these "quasi-acrobatic steps." *An Evening with Gene Kelly*, 6:30.

38. See John O'Connor, "TV Reviews; 'American Film Institute Salute to Gene Kelly,'" *New York Times*, May 7, 1985, C22.

39. Reynolds, *Debbie: My Life*, 73–74.

40. Ibid., 40–41.

41. Ibid., 48.

42. The films were *The Daughter of Rosie O'Grady, Three Little Words*, and *Two Weeks with Love*. Reynolds also earned $15,000 in royalties on record sales for a duet with Carleton Carpenter featured in *Two Weeks with Love*, "Aba Daba Honeymoon." Ibid., 55–76.

43. "[Before An American in Paris] I had never spoken in my life on the stage and having to act out loud was a nightmare for me." Leslie Caron, quoted in Simon Hattenstone, "'I am very shy. It's amazing I became a movie star': Leslie Caron at 90 on love, art and addiction," *Guardian*, June 21, 2021, accessed April 18, 2023, at: https://www.theguardian.com/lifeandstyle/2021/jun/21/i-am-very-shy-its-amazing-i-became-a-movie-star-leslie-caron-at-90-on-love-art-and-addiction.

44. *What a Glorious Feeling*, 16:13.

45. Hedda Hopper, "Mankiewicz Prepares Dr. Praetorius Story," *Los Angeles Times*, October 16, 1950, B6.

46. Comden and Green, *Singin' in the Rain* (1972), foreword, x.

47. Edwin Schallert, "Drama: Kirk Douglas Angling for Comedy; Gene Kelly Again Will Codirect," *Los Angeles Times*, March 3, 1951, 9.

48. Hedda Hopper, "Drama: 'Price Tag' Affixed by Lupino and Young," *Los Angeles Times*, April 3, 1951, B6.

49. Fordin, *MGM's Greatest Musicals*, 354.

50. Dabholkar and Hess, "*Singin' in the Rain*," 52.

51. Hirschhorn, *Gene Kelly*, 181–82.

52. "The Marrying Kind," AFI Catalog of Feature Films online.

53. Dabholkar and Hess, "*Singin' in the Rain*," 53.

54. Ibid.
55. Curtis Lee Hanson, "An Interview with Gene Kelly," *Cinema* 3, no. 4 (December 1966): 26. Quoted in Dabholkar and Hess, 53.
56. Hirschhorn, *Gene Kelly*, 182.
57. "*Singin' in the Rain* 50th Anniversary," 16:45.
58. Charisse and Martin, *The Two of Us*, 201–2; cited in Dabholkar and Hess, "*Singin' in the Rain*," 294n10. Charisse also discusses her casting in "*Singin' in the Rain* 50th Anniversary," 11:56.
59. Philip Scheuer, "Rita Moreno's Principal Aim Is to Be Bullfighter," *Los Angeles Times*, October 26, 1952, E1.
60. Dave Gil de Rubio, "The Many Lives of Rita Moreno: Veteran Performer Reflects in Latest Documentary," *East Bay Express*, October 5, 2021, accessed online on March 30, 2023, at: https://eastbayexpress.com/the-many-lives-of-rita-moreno/.
61. Hannah Lewis, "*Love Me Tonight (1932)* and the Development of the Integrated Film Musical," *Musical Quarterly* 100, no. 1 (Spring 2017): 4.
62. Bosley Crowther, "'Singin' in the Rain,' Starring Gene Kelly, Ushers In Spring at the Music Hall," *New York Times*, March 28, 1952, 27.
63. Jane Feuer "The Self-Reflexive Musical and the Myth of Entertainment," in *Film Genre Reader II*, ed. Barry Keith Grant (Austin: University of Texas Press, 1995), 443.
64. Ibid., 444.
65. Ibid.
66. Feuer, *The Hollywood Musical*, 2nd ed. 1993, 35–42.
67. Donen's complex montages constitute, according to Hannah Lewis, a third form of integration, "storytelling through . . . cinematic techniques, a kind of reflexive stylization that is in tension with the ideal of [narrative] integration." Lewis, "*Love Me Tonight*," 4.
68. Dabholkar and Hess also identify Thompson as Gene Kelly's assistant. Dabholkar and Hess, "*Singin' in the Rain*," 102.
69. Comden and Green, "Singin' in the Rain," 1950-10-14 Temporary Complete Script, Comden and Green Papers, Box 9, Folder 6, NYPL, 44.
70. Vincent Canby, "A Joyously Indestructible Movie Returns," *New York Times*, May 4, 1975, D15.
71. Wollen, *Singin' in the Rain*, 11.
72. "Gene Kelly, Rita Hayworth & Phil Silvers— Make Way for Tomorrow," YouTube, February 4, 2012, https://www.youtube.com/watch?v = lNS5UXpFC9M.
73. Hirschhorn, *Gene Kelly*, 182.
74. The railroad stations were shot on Lot 2 at the Small Town Railroad Depot. See Bingen et al., *MGM: Hollywood's Greatest Backlot*, 160.
75. Comden and Green, "Singin' in the Rain," 1950-10-14 Temporary Complete Script, Comden and Green Papers, Box 9, Folder 6, NYPL, 6.
76. See "Draft of new finale by Joseph Fields" (not used), July 26, 1951, Turner/MGM Scripts, Folder 1241, AL. Fields's version of the finale incorporates movements like sliding down a rope, a trick Kelly performed onscreen in *The Pirate*. Elsewhere in *Singin'*, film footage from Kelly's sword fights in *The Three Musketeers* is recycled. See Dabholkar and Hess, "*Singin'*," 140–42.
77. Comden and Green, "Singin' in the Rain," 1951-04-11 clean script with inserted pages dated up to 1951-7-20, Betty Comden Papers, Box 12, Folder 11, NYPL, 97.
78. Panel Discussion, "Singin' in the Rain 50th Anniversary," at 5:54.
79. Comden and Green, *Singin' in the Rain* (1972), 72. The word "hasn't" appears instead of the word "ain't" in both late first draft and second draft "OK" scripts; see 1950-10-14 Temporary Complete Script, Comden and Green Papers, Box 9, Folder 6, NYPL, 84; and 1951-04-11 clean script with inserted pages dated up to 1951-7-20, Betty Comden Papers, Box 12, Folder 11, NYPL, 91.
80. Reynolds employed the actor's friend, onions, to elicit copious tears. "What a Glorious Feeling," 25:10.
81. For example, the last two and half minutes of *Singin' in the Rain*, with Reynolds's own voice substituted for Betty Noyes and instrumental underscoring substituted for the final choral rendition of "Lucky Star," accessed December 10, 2022, https://www.youtube.com/watch?v = freaNntFqW4.
82. There exists, however, a flawless performance of the difficult passage by ghost singer Marjorie Lane (dubbing Eleanor Powell, who sits, daydreaming, in an empty theater) late in *Broadway Melody of 1936.*
83. See quote in the preface from Eugene Archer, "Museum to Show Gene Kelly Films: 9 of Dancer's Movies Listed—Reception to Honor Him," *New York Times*, August 10, 1962, 11.

Chapter 3: Choreography and Cuts

1. Gene Kelly, quoted in Silverman, *Dancing on the Ceiling*, 32.
2. Wollen, *Singin' in the Rain*, 34 and 38–39. Kelly performed "Be a Clown" with the Nicholas Brothers in *The Pirate*. See chapters 2 and 5 regarding controversies around Kelly and O'Connor's uses of flash steps without direct attribution.
3. Reynolds did study ballet both at Warner Brothers and MGM. "I loved it but I couldn't do it." Debbie Reynolds, *My Life*, 62.
4. Kelly danced with a translucent shadow of himself in *Cover Girl* (1944, his first cinematic collaboration with Donen) and with a cartoon mouse in *Anchors Aweigh* (1945). See Dabholkar and Hess, *Gene Kelly*, 128 and 150.
5. *What a Glorious Feeling*, 25:21.
6. Charness whittled this list down, omitting the title sequence version of "Singin' in the Rain," Kelly's slow dance with Reynolds to "You Were Meant for Me," and their cinematic movements away and toward one another in the finale, "You Are My Lucky Star." Casey Charness, "Hollywood Cine-Dance," 100.
7. Watson appeared as Bing Crosby's energetic agent in *Going Hollywood* (1933), a film featuring a number of songs by Brown and Freed and an orchestra led by Lennie Hayton. Watson worked on Broadway in *Irene* in 1919 and seven other Broadway shows throughout the 1920s. "Bobby Watson," *Internet Broadway Database*, n.d., https://www.ibdb.com/broadway-cast-staff/bobby-watson-64210.
8. Charness described the number as possessing "hardly a smidgen of dance content" and plausibly suggests that Donen and Kelly meant it as a critique, "a kind of left-handed salute to Busby Berkeley's thyroid visions." Charness, "Hollywood Cine-Dance," 100.
9. Berkeley also directed Kelly's film debut, *For Me and My Gal* (1942).
10. Berkeley used this shot in films as early as *Whoopee* (1930). See James Layton and David Pierce, *The Dawn of Technicolor, 1915–1935* (Rochester, NY: George Eastman House, 2015), 10.
11. Comden and Green, "Singin' in the Rain," 1951-04-11 clean script with revisions to 1951-7-20, Betty Comden Papers, Box 12, Folder 11, NYPL, 44–45.
12. Fordin, *MGM's Greatest Musicals*, 359.
13. Ibid.
14. Dabholkar and Hess, "Singin' in the Rain," 102.
15. See Dabholkar and Hess, "Singin' in the Rain," 161–69, for a detailed account of the ballet's production.
16. "What a Glorious Feeling," 26:06 and 28:06. These were probably not stages 5 and 6, which were typically left set up as a theater and were where the proscenium stage scenes in *Singin'* and many other musicals were shot. See Bingen et al., *MGM: Hollywood's Greatest Backlot*, 103.
17. Dabholkar and Hess, "Singin'," 168.
18. Lloyd Whitesell created an analogous but quite different table as part of a fascinating discussion of the ballet in his book *Wonderful Design*, 98.
19. Apparently the wig was actually modeled on one made for Pola Negri, another silent film star, who appeared in a variety of different hairstyles during her career. Dabholkar and Hess, "Singin'," 160.
20. Talya Alon has suggested that Marlene Dietrich's performance of "Falling in Love Again" in *Die Blaue Engel* was the inspiration for this scene. Alon, "It's Raining Films: Intertextuality in *Singin' in the Rain*," *Literature/Film Quarterly* 45, no. 3 (Summer 2017): 9–10.
21. See Michael Koresky, "An American in Paris and Gigi," *Reverse Shot* (Museum of the Moving Image, February 21, 2014), accessed online on December 1, 2022, at: https://reverseshot.org/features/221/an-american-in-paris-and-gigi.
22. For example, see Urban's design for the palace steps in *Turandot* (1924) for a 1926 production at the Metropolitan Opera, at: https://dlc.library.columbia.edu/catalog/ldpd:156379/details.
23. Dabholkar and Hess, "Singin' in the Rain," 174.
24. Albert Johnson, "Conversation with Roger Edens" *Sight and Sound* 27, no. 4 (Spring 1958): 179.
25. Casper, *Stanley Donen*, 34; quoted in Wollen, *Singin'*, 59.
26. Stuart Hall and Paddy Whannel, *The Popular Arts* (London: Hutchinson, 1964), xx; quoted in Wollen, *Singin'*, 59.
27. Kerry Kelly Novick, quoted in Kara Gardner, "Revealing the Subconscious: The Dream Ballet in Movie Musicals," in Broomfield-McHugh, ed., *The Oxford Handbook of the Hollywood*

Musical, 53–54; from a longer interview with Novick posted online at: https://circulatingnow.
nlm.nih.gov/2014/03/12/on-combat-fatigue-irritability-kerry-kelly-novick-part-1/.

28. Broomfield-McHugh, 48.
29. "Singin' in the Rain 50th Anniversary," 13:58.
30. Kelly wanted a "seductive yet cold . . . vamp" according to Dabholkar and Hess, *"Singin' in the Rain,"* 160.
31. Letter to Dore Schary from Joseph I. Breen, January 3, 1952, "'Singin' in the Rain,' 1952," Motion Picture Association of America, Production Code Administration Records, Margaret Herrick Library.
32. Censor's reports, "'Singin' in the Rain,' 1952," ibid. See also Dabholkar and Hess, *"Singin' in the Rain,"* 180–82.
33. "What a Glorious Feeling," 30:15.
34. Ibid., 30:16.
35. Dabholkar and Hess, *"Singin' in the Rain,"* 100–101 and 286n44.
36. Betty Comden and Adolph Green, "Singin' in the Rain," "OK" script, Betty Comden Papers, Box 12, Folder 11, NYPL, 45.
37. J. J. Cohn, "Eliminations Made from 'Singing in the Rain,'" memo to Freed and Donen dated April 11, 1952, Freed Papers, Box 23, Folder 1, USC. See *Singin' in the Rain*, 2-DVD set, for photos and audio recordings of the two scenes.
38. Dabholkar and Hess make similar points about the solos being duplicative and "repetitive." Dabholkar and Hess, *"Singin' in the Rain,"* 174.
39. Mike Connolly, "Rambling Reporter," *Hollywood Reporter* 118, no. 22 (March 14, 1952): 2.
40. Dabholkar and Hess, *"Singin' in the Rain,"* 173.
41. Anonymous, "500 Prints for 'Rain,'" *Hollywood Reporter* 118, no. 21 (March 13, 1952): 6.
42. The video and audio are included on the 2002 2-DVD release of *Singin'*. See also Debbie Reynolds singing "You Are My Lucky Star"– Outtake, accessed December 2, 2022, https://www.youtube.com/watch?v=CD1j4buZnJI.
43. Still photos of the set for Don's bedroom are reproduced in *What a Glorious Feeling* (2002), 29.27 and 29.34.
44. Silverman, *Dancing on the Ceiling*, 158.
45. Hirschhorn, *Gene Kelly*, 189.
46. Behlmer, *America's Favorite Movies*, 268.
47. "Don—after party—'All I Do Is Dream of You,'" production April–July 1951, Arthur Freed Papers, Box 22, Folder 15, AL. The number is identified more accurately as "Gene Dreams of Kathy" in a much later inventory of all the music cues for the film. See "SINGIN' IN THE RAIN / (Feature) / (Music Report and Footage) (March 15 [penciled in] 17, 1952)," Turner/MGM Scripts, Folder S-1242, AL.
48. The audio track is included on the 2-CD 2002 release of the film's soundtrack and outtakes (disc 1, track 5). End of Party Scene including a fragment of the cut version of "All I Do Is Dream of You," accessed December 3, 2022, https://www.youtube.com/watch?v=GQaKNdyj1Ro.
49. *Singin' in the Rain*, original motion picture soundtrack, liner notes. See also table 4.1.
50. Anonymous, "Singin' in the Rain. From the M-G-M picture," Notice of a new publication of song and orchestration sheet music by Metro Goldwyn Mayer, *Notes* 9, no. 3 (June 1952): 505.
51. As mentioned, this phrase resembles the opening phrase of Edward "Duke" Ellington's composition "In a Sentimental Mood" (1935), as does the underscoring for "Dignity, always dignity" at 4:35.
52. A quotation from Stravinsky's *Petrushka* (1911) appears at 0:40 in the high winds, twice.
53. Betty Comden, quoted in William Baer, *Classic American Films: Conversations with the Screenwriters* (Westport, CT: Praeger, 2008), 9.
54. Betty Comden in conversation with critic Michael Riedel in 1993, included in a retrospective episode of the television series *Theatre Talk* titled "Remembering Betty Comden" (CUNY-TV and WGBH, October 4, 2007).
55. Rodgers and Hammerstein's norms included the idea that "the songs [should] flow directly from the dialogue." See Geoffrey Block, "Integration," 97.
56. Wollen offers a spirited defense of the ballet, citing the criticism of Victor Shklovsky and invoking works by Chaucer, Boccaccio, Cervantes, and Melville as comparably digressive. Wollen, *Singin'*, 59.

Chapter 4: Music and Sound

1. Gene Kelly in an interview with Jerome Delameter and Paddy Whannel on November 20, 1973, quoted in Delameter, *Dance in the Hollywood Musical*, 223–24.
2. Ibid., 223.
3. Ibid., 223–24. Chaplin worked on *On the Town* and *An American in Paris* but not on *Singin'*. Previn joined MGM in 1953.
4. John Wilson, quoted in Richard Hindley, "Conrad Salinger—M-G-M Arranger Supreme," *Robert Farnon Society Magazine* (September 2003), accessed April 30, 2023 at: https://www.robertfarnonsociety.org.uk/index.php/legends/conrad-salinger.
5. Todd Decker, *Music Makes Me*, 131.
6. Ibid., 136.
7. *Singin' in the Rain*, original motion picture soundtrack, liner notes.
8. Reynolds also worked part-time as a DJ at a radio station in Los Angeles long associated with Warner Brothers, KFWB. Reynolds, *My Life*, 53.
9. In what is a roughly comparable practice, many young singers in more recent years have had their voices routinely retuned and acoustically retailored by audio wizards behind the scenes. Reynolds dubbed her own numbers the very next year in *I Love Melvin* (1953).
10. Nathan Platte, "Performing Prestige: American Cinema Orchestras, 1910–1958," in *Oxford Handbook of Film Music Studies*, ed. David Neumeyer (New York: Oxford University Press, 2014), 634.
11. Ibid., 630. See one of these films, *The Jubilee Overture* (1954), a medley of eleven songs beginning with "Singin' in the Rain" and including "Broadway Rhythm" and "Temptation"; accessed October 26, 2022, https://www.youtube.com/watch?v = eMqPet2erWw.
12. Platte, 635.
13. See Stephen Handzo, "Glossary of Film Sound Technology," in *Film Sound Theory and Practice*, ed. Elisabeth Weis and John Belton (New York: Columbia University Press, 1985), 390–91.
14. List of Music Credits included at the end of Continuity Script, Turner/MGM Scripts, Folder S-1242.
15. "Production April-July 1951," Arthur Freed Papers, Box 22, Folder 15, USC.
16. Dabholkar and Hess suggest that the trio may have been intended for a scene being shot for Zelda's new film; that spot was filled by "Beautiful Girl" on a page inserted into the "OK" script on May 23. Comden and Green, *Singin'* "OK" Script, Betty Comden Papers, Box 12, Folder 11, NYPL, 44–48. See also Dabholkar and Hess, *Singin' in the Rain*, 70–71.
17. The song is by Freed and Brown; the dream sequence occurs at 32:41–39:23 in *Going Hollywood* and the trio begins at 35:55.
18. "Ebertfest Flashback: Donald O'Connor on 'Singin' in the Rain'" [interview transcript] (website post, April 27, 2003), accessed October 24, 2022, https://www.rogerebert.com/festivals/ebertfest-flashback-donald-oconnor-on-singin-in-the-rain.
19. Silverman, *Stanley Donen*, 156n.
20. "Singin' in the Rain: [Assistant Director's Reports], 1951 April 2–1952 Jan 10," Arthur Freed Papers, Box 2, series of folders, USC.
21. Ibid.
22. Debbie Reynolds's narration in "What a Glorious Feeling"; see also Dabholkar and Hess, *Singin' in the Rain*, 82.
23. "What a Glorious Feeling."
24. Ibid.
25. "Singin' in The Rain: [Assistant Director's Reports]."
26. Ibid., although a full shooting schedule, dated June 5, 1951, had projected November 9 as a completion date. Arthur Freed Papers, Box 23, Folder 1, USC.
27. Fordin, *MGM's Greatest Musicals*, 358.
28. Ibid.
29. Regarding Kelly and O'Connor's dubbing see Dabholkar and Hess, *Singin' in the Rain*, 151. Regarding Carol Haney, Conrad Kahn, and Nina Simone's preparatory work on "wet taps," see Helen Hanson, "Looking for Lela Simone," 833–34.
30. Dabholkar and Hess, *Singin' in the Rain*, 151.
31. Ibid., 151 and 261.
32. Comden and Green, *Singin' in the Rain*, foreword (1972), vi.
33. Ibid. See the floor plan illustrating the offices of Edens, Freed, Simone, and others reproduced in Fordin, *MGM's Greatest Musicals*, 120.

34. Silverman suggests that MGM's *Two Girls on Broadway* (1940) also "rehashed the essential plot of the first *Melody*." Silverman, *Dancing on the Ceiling*, 145n.
35. The screenplay for *Broadway Melody of 1936* was co-authored by Jack MacGowan, author of *Excess Baggage*, and Dore Schary, who eventually displaced Mayer as head of production at MGM in 1952. The songs in the fourth film in the series, *Broadway Melody of 1940*, were written by Cole Porter.
36. *Broadway Melody of 1938*, AFI Catalog of Feature Films online. See also Johnson, "Conversation with Roger Edens, 179–80.
37. In an early instance of smell-o-vision, the scent of orange blossoms wafted through selected theaters during an earlier color sequence, a "Technicolor Ballet" set in an onstage orange grove accompanied by Gus Edwards and Joe Goodwin's song "Orange Blossom Time." See Roger Fristo, "The Broadway Revue of 1929," TCM.com, October 23, 2007, https://www.tcm.com/tcmdb/title/211/the-hollywood-revue-of-1929#articles-reviews
38. *San Francisco*, AFI Catalog of Feature Films online.
39. Popularized by a song of the same name, "The Charleston" (1923), written by James P. Johnson for the Broadway show *Runnin' Wild*. For more details see Robert Rawlins, "'Charleston,' The Golden Gate Orchestra" (Library of Congress, National Recording Preservation Board website, n.d.), accessed on August 10, 2022 at: https://www.loc.gov/static/programs/national-recording-preservation-board/documents/Charleston.pdf.
40. "Temptation" (lyrics by Arthur Freed, music by Nacio Herb Brown), sung by Bing Crosby, orchestra conducted by Lennie Hayton, recorded in Los Angeles October 22, 1933. Brunswick 6695, 78 rpm record, 1933. Accessed August 9, 2022, https://www.youtube.com/watch?v = 3qAshUH7ySc.
41. *Going Hollywood*, AFI Catalog of Feature Films online.
42. Walter Frisch, *Arlen and Harburg's* Over the Rainbow (New York: Oxford University Press, 2017), 58.
43. *The Broadway Melody of 1929*, AFI Catalog of Feature Films online.
44. "Background of Melody Now Passé—Theme Songs Introduced to Carry on Story and Action Beyond Spoken Dialogue," *Los Angeles Times*, March 3, 1929, C33.
45. Note: All the musical examples in this chapter are transposed into the common key of C.
46. Kelly chose to vary this phrase in performance, singing different pitches not in the sheet music (6:01),
47. Kelly, interviewed by Gavin Millar in *An Evening with Gene Kelly*.
48. Ibid.
49. Anonymous, "Composer Cherishes First Hit Written At 10 Years Of Age," *Los Angeles Times*, January 9, 1927, C27.
50. The song appears twice in *The Pirate* (1948): Kelly's trio with Fayard and Harold Nicholas, and the film's finale, Kelly's duet with Judy Garland.
51. Clover, "Dancin' in the Rain," 722 and (in reprint) 157.
52. Michael Feinstein, *Nice Work If You Can Get It: My Life in Rhythm and Rhyme* (New York: Hyperion, 1995), 316. On the same page Feinstein reported that actor and songwriter Kay Thompson, who worked as a vocal coach at MGM, also confronted Freed about the obvious resemblance between the two songs, asking reproachingly, "How can you do that?" Stanley Donen, quoted in Fordin, *MGM's Greatest Musicals*, 359.
53. Jonas Westover, "'Be a Clown' and 'Make 'Em Laugh': Comic Timing, Rhythm, and Donald O'Connor's Face," in *Sounding Funny: Sound and Comedy Cinema*, ed. Mark Evans and Philip Heyward (Sheffield, UK and Bristol, CT: Equinox Publishing, 2016), 122–47.
54. "Make 'Em Laugh" is written out in common time, 4/4, rather than cut time, the original time signature, 2/2; the note durations are equivalent in either time signature.
55. SINGIN' IN THE RAIN (1952), 1952-03-17 Complete script divided into 6 reels for "(Dialogue Cutting Continuity) / (Film Editor: Adrienne Fazan, A.C.E.)," stamped "DEPARTMENT COPY" and "FILE COPY," Turner/MGM Scripts, Folder S-1242, AL. No number. At end of script, a list of music by reel, with composer (and lyricist, if applicable) listed. Folder contents in full: "dialogue cutting continuity" by Adrienne Fazan (editor, 111 pages), "music report and footage," March 17, 1952 (13 pages), "musical notes" by Lela Simone, October 20, 1951 (11 pages), and "international broadcast music" (7 pages, undated).
56. Ibid., narrative for Reel 6, page 11.
57. Ibid., Music Report and Footage (March 15 [penciled in] 17, 1952).
58. Dabholkar and Hess, *Singin' in the Rain*, 151.

59. Milton Lustig, music editor, in *The Hollywood Sound*, a film by Joshua Waletzky (NHK/Arte/ WNET, 1995), 29:04.

60. David Raksin and John Mauceri demonstrate and discuss the process in *The Hollywood Sound*, 30:56. For another example see Richard Bellis, "Streamers and Punches," YouTube, January 15, 2019, accessed August 8, 2022, https://www.youtube.com/watch?v = ubySE_cRXMw.

61. "SINGIN' IN THE RAIN (1952)," Turner/MGM Scripts, Folder S-1242, AL.

62. Doug Galloway, "Jacque Mapes, Studio Art Director and Set Decorator" [obituary], *Variety*, May 7, 2002, accessed April 22, 2023, https://variety.com/2002/scene/people-news/jacque-mapes-1117866564/.

63. The patter, with the authors listed, was submitted to the censorship office on May 21, 1951. Motion Picture Association of America, Production Code Administration Records, Margaret Herrick Library.

64. Ibid.

65. Kelly is quoted in Delamater, *Dance in the Hollywood Musical*, 136.

66. See James Fuld, *The Book of World-Famous Music: Classical, Popular, and Folk* (Mineola, NY: Dover Publications, 1995 [1966]), 591–92. The tune was originally published as "Zip Coon" (1834), making it another of the racialized moments in the film discussed by Clover and Chin and the kind of erasure documented by Gottschild. See chapters 3 and 5 for discussions of borrowings from African American dancers by Kelly and O'Connor.

67. Gershwin borrowed the theme (perhaps via intermediary versions) from *La Mattchiche* (1905) by Charles Borel-LeClerc. Ibid., 358–59; see also Howard Pollack, *George Gershwin: His Life and Work* (Berkeley: University of California Press, 2006), 434–35.

68. Fordin, *MGM's Greatest Musicals*, 351.

69. "Don's solo song and dance to 'Singin' in the Rain,'" accessed December 17, 2022, https://www.youtube.com/watch?v = D1ZYhVpdXbQ.

70. Lela Simone, "'SINGIN' IN THE RAIN' / Production 1546 / Music Notes," October 20, 1951, Turner/MGM Scripts, Folder S-1242, AL. The sound effect sounds more like a rattle along an actual iron fence than a xylophone.

71. See biography in "Finding Aid for the Arthur Freed Papers" (Online Archive of California), accessed December 16, 2022, https://oac.cdlib.org/findaid/ark:/13030/c8vt1zpg/entire_text/. See also an announcement that Brown had been hired at MGM, Anonymous, "Pictures—Coast Notes," *Variety*, September 26, 1928, 24.

72. Denfeld, "Future Hollywood producer Arthur Freed." This essay is the principal source for Freed's biography as related here.

73. "New Tin Pan Alley is In West—Some Jazz Composers Who Are Turning Tunes Into Money," *Los Angeles Times*, June 18, 1922, Part III, 16.

74. "Song Writer Now Manager of Playhouse," *Los Angeles Times*, April 13, 1924, 22. These songs, like many of Freed's early titles, were published by Sherman & Clay, a publisher and music store chain based in San Francisco.

75. "Los Angeles Theatres; Grand Theater," accessed December 10, 2022, https://losangelest heatres.blogspot.com/2018/11/grand-theatre.html; and "Los Angeles, 1909; Theatres and Amusements; Walker, The, Grand, Bet. 7th and 8th . . . K9," panoramic map, Library of Congress, https://www.loc.gov/item/2005632465/. The six-story building was constructed in 1908 and demolished in 1946; the site is now just a block from the Metro Center subway station.

76. The Music Box, renamed the Fonda Theatre, is still in operation; see Alan Michelson, "DeHaven, Carter, Music Box Theatre, Hollywood, Los Angeles, CA (1926)," *Pacific Coast Architecture Database*, http://pcad.lib.washington.edu/building/7588/.

77. Doris Eaton Travis, *The Days We Danced*, 134.

78. "Amusement Project Under Construction—Home Gardens Will Have New Dancing Establishment And Offices Local Correspondence," *Los Angeles Times*, July 22, 1923, V7.

79. Travis, *The Days We Danced*, 132.

80. "Tune Written for Fill-in Becomes National Success," *Los Angeles Times*, May 8, 1927, 21.

81. Travis, *The Days We Danced*, 141.

82. Ibid., 143.

83. Anne Shannon Monroe, *Singing in the Rain* (Garden City, NY: Doubleday, Page & Co., 1926), 2–3. Editions of the book with both 1926 and 1927 appearing as the copyright date exist. Portions of the book originally appeared in *Good Housekeeping* magazine. See also Nancy Dunis, "Singin' in the Rain—Anne Shannon Monroe's Story," *Lake Oswego Review*, February 20, 2023, accessed

April 7, 2023, at: https://www.lakeoswegoreview.com/lifestyle/singin-in-the-rain-anne-shan non-monroes-story/article_03ed096a-af02-11ed-9f49-f7b5d27cc9ec.html.

84. Dabholkar and Hess, *Singin' in the Rain*, 62 and 13; although the date provided there for Monroe's book is that of the last reprint (1936) rather than the first edition (1926).

Chapter 5: Reception History

1. For a more comprehensive account of the marketing of the film and subsequent reviews world-wide, see Dabholkar and Hess, *Singin' in the Rain*, 175–88.
2. Bosley Crowther, "'Singin' in the Rain,' Starring Gene Kelly, Ushers In Spring at the Music Hall; A Psychologist's Life in Prison, 'My Six Convicts,' With Mitchell, at Astor," *New York Times*, March 28, 1952, 27; Philip Scheuer, "'Singin' in Rain' Satirizes Silents," *Los Angeles Times*, April 10, 1952, B9; and Otis Guernsey Jr., "'Singin' in the Rain': Sparkling Spring Musical," *New York Herald Tribune*, March 28, 1952, 13.
3. Vincent Canby, "Film View: A Joyously Indestructible Movie Returns," *New York Times*, May 4, 1975, D15.
4. Altman, ed., *Genre, the Musical*; Feuer, *The Hollywood Musical*.
5. Fordin, *MGM's Greatest Musicals*; Wollen, *Singin' in the Rain*; and Dabholkar and Hess, "*Singin' in the Rain*."
6. "5 New Pix Steady B'way; 'Singin' Sock $146,000," *Variety*, April 2, 1951, 9.
7. "'Singin' $1,500,000 Paces April B.O.," *Variety*, May 7, 1952, 4.
8. Dabholkar and Hess, *Singin' in the Rain*, 188; Behlmer, *America's Favorite Movies*, 268; Fordin, *M-G-M's Greatest Musicals*, 362; Silverman, *Stanley Donen*, 155; and "What a Glorious Feeling."
9. No MGM films made before 1986 were included in Amazon's purchase of MGM's remaining library in 2021. See Brooks Barnes et al., "James Bond, Meet Jeff Bezos: Amazon Makes $8.45 Billion Deal for MGM," *New York Times*, May 26, 2021, B1. Warner Media merged with Discovery Inc. in 2022. See John Koblin, "In Hollywood, a New Giant Joins the Ranks," *New York Times*, April 9, 2022, B1.
10. Display Ad, "Singin' in the Rain," *New York Herald Tribune*, March 27, 1952, 21. Richard Kluger, quoted in Sam Roberts, "Recalling a 'Writer's Paper' as a Name Fades," *New York Times*, March 7, 2013, A21.
11. Display Ad, "Singin' in the Rain," *New York Times*, March 27, 1952, 35.
12. Charisse's leg is propped against the outside of Kelly's leg rather than resting across his crotch as in the film. The vast veil is only faintly visible, flying at a different angle. Presumably the source was a still photograph shot for publicity purposes, not the film itself. The analogous moment in the second duet occurs at 1:25:45 in the film.
13. The hour-long live stage show included a "beautiful, far-famed Cathedral pageant" celebrating Easter with symphony orchestra and theater organ, a secular show "celebrating Springtide frolics and finery" including a fashion show, a visiting ballet troupe (the D'Andrea Dancers), a young operatic tenor (Edward Ruhl), the Swiss juggler Béla Kremo, and "the famed Rockettes in glamorous precision." Display Ad, *New York Herald Tribune*, 21.
14. Ibid.
15. The other Oscars awarded to the creators of *An American in Paris* were: Color Art Direction–Set Decoration (Cedric Gibbons, Preston Ames, Edwin B. Willis, and Keogh Gleason), Color Cinematography (Alfred Gilks and John Alton), Color Costume Design (Orry-Kelly, Walter Plunkett, and Irene Sharaff), Music—Scoring of a Musical Picture (Johnny Green and Saul Chaplin—Donald O'Connor presented the award), Writing—Story and Screenplay (Alan Jay Lerner). Arthur Freed received the Thalberg award. Gene Kelly received an honorary award "in appreciation of his versatility . . . and brilliant achievements in the art of choreography on film." Donen accepted the award in Kelly's absence. "The 24th Academy Awards," Academy of Motion Picture and Arts and Sciences, March 20, 1952, https://www.oscars.org/oscars/cer emonies/1952.
16. "Films for Children," *New York Times*, March 27, 1952, 36.
17. Various Small Display Ads, *New York Herald Tribune*, March 27, 1952, 21. Some older films still running in neighborhood houses were rated as suitable for children, including *The Lavender Hill Mob* (1951), and *Passion for Life [L'École Buissonnière*, also known as *Skipping School]* (1949). *Viva Zapata*, which opened in February 1952, was approved but only for children at least thirteen years old. See "Films for Children," 36.
18. "Flesh and Fury," AFI Catalog of Feature Films online.
19. "11 Films Opening in N.Y. This Week," *Hollywood Reporter*, March 25, 1952, 4.

20. See *Pal Joey*, second Broadway production (January 3, 1952–April 18, 1953), *Internet Broadway Database*. Lang was in the original cast of *Fancy Free* (1944), the ballet precursor to *On the Town* (1944).

21. "The King and I: Opening Night Cast," and "Gigi," *Internet Broadway Database*.

22. Louis Calta, "'The Grass Harp' to Open Tonight," *New York Times*, March 27, 1952, 35.

23. All quotes in this paragraph are from Crowther, "'Singin' in the Rain,'" 27.

24. Crowther, "An April Shower; Rain of Refreshing Pictures Descends Upon Local Film Theatres," *New York Times*, April 6, 1952, X1.

25. Otis Guernsey Jr., "'Singin' in the Rain': Sparkling Spring Musical," *New York Herald Tribune*, March 28, 1952, 13.

26. Guernsey, "A Bright Easter Package: 'Singin in the Rain,'" *New York Herald Tribune*, April 6, 1952, D1.

27. Herbert Kupferberg, "The World's Biggest Movie Studio Dazzles a Tourist," *New York Herald Tribune*, April 6, 1952, D1.

28. Walter Terry, "The Dance World: Kelly's Exhilarating Dance Tonic for April," *New York Herald Tribune*, April 13, 1952, D4.

29. Otis Guernsey Jr., "The 10 Best: Movie Critic Presents His Annual Laurels; Top Movies of '52," *New York Herald Tribune*, December 28, 1952, D1.

30. Alex Barris, "On the Screen: 'Singin' in the Rain,'" *Toronto Globe and Mail*, May 27, 1952, 12.

31. K.C.S., "Damp Daze in Venice—it could have been fine," *Dublin Times Pictorial*, January 24, 1953, 5.

32. Our London Film Critic, "New Films in London," *Manchester Guardian*, April 12, 1952, 3.

33. Classified Ad, "Singin' in the Rain," *Manchester Guardian*, August 14, 1952, 1.

34. Thanks to Dominic Broomfield-McHugh for supplying me with a rare copy of a four-page-long UK pressbook, from a 1961 MGM promotional campaign for a "re-presentation" of the film.

35. Ronald Haver, "Singin' in the Rain," *Criterion Collection*, December 12, 1988, accessed August 29, 2022, https://www.criterion.com/current/posts/817-singin-in-the-rain.

36. "Singin' in the Rain," in program notes for the Berkeley Film Society, screened at the Cinema-Guild and Studio, Berkeley, CA, May–June 1958, unpaged, accessed August 29, 2022, from the University of California Berkeley Art Museum and Pacific Film Archive, https://cinefiles.bampfa.berkeley.edu/catalog/58241. Haver cites Kael as the author of these notes; see Haver, "Singin' in the Rain."

37. Pauline Kael, *I Lost It at the Movies* (Boston: Little, Brown, 1965), 142.

38. Comden and Green, *Singin' in the Rain* (1972), xii.

39. Richard Schickel, "A Way of Seeing a Picture: I Lost It at the Movies by Pauline Kael," *New York Times*, March 14, 1965, BR6.

40. Eugene Archer, "Museum to Show Gene Kelly Films: 9 of Dancer's Movies Listed—Reception to Honor Him," *New York Times*, August 10, 1962, 11.

41. Jon Gartenberg, quoted in Neil Genzlinger, "Adrienne Mancia, Influential Film Curator, Dies at 95," *New York Times*, December 21, 2022, A19.

42. In addition to Altman, ed., *Genre*, and Feuer, *The Hollywood Musical*, see Mordden, *The Hollywood Musical*; Delamater, *Dance in the Hollywood Musical*; and Behlmer, *America's Favorite Movies*.

43. Haver, "Singin' in the Rain."

44. Ibid.

45. Ibid.

46. Canby, "Film View," D15.

47. Ibid.

48. Ibid.

49. Ibid.

50. Ibid.

51. Ibid.

52. "Places to Take the City Youngster," *New York Times*, May 8, 1975, 45.

53. "il s'agit bien, cette fois, d'un film d'auteur ce qui est rare dans ce genre de productions [it is indeed, this time, an *auteur* film which is rare in this kind of production]"; Claude Chabrol, "Que Ma Joie Demeure," 55.

54. "*Chantons sous la pluie* qui est, de bout en bout, absolument et résolument une oeuvre de cinéaste [*Singin' in the Rain* which is, from start to finish, absolutely and resolutely the work of a filmmaker]." Ibid.

55. Kelly, "Gene Kelly: The Performing Auteur," 137.
56. Ibid., 136.
57. Chin, "Michael Jackson's Panther Dance," 59.
58. Ibid., 58 and 69.
59. Nils Grosch and Jonas Mensch, "Anmerkungen zur musikalischen Dramaturgie und Struktur von [Notes on the musical dramaturgy and structure of] Singin' in the Rain," and Ralph Poole, "'I cayn't make love to a bush!' Lina Lamont und die Austreibung weiblicher Komik [and the exorcism of female comedy] in Singin' in the Rain," in Grosch and Brügge, "Singin' in the Rain," 11–26 and 133–56.
60. Nils Grosch, "Musical Comedy, Pastiche and the Challenge of 'Rewriting,'" 157.
61. de Lucas, "Dancing Happiness," 62–63.
62. Ireland, "Singin' Over Rainbows," 123.
63. Westover, "'Be a Clown' and 'Make 'Em Laugh,'" 123.
64. Ibid.
65. Ibid., 145.
66. Ibid., 143.
67. Nadel, Demographic Angst, 32.
68. Whitesell, Wonderful Design, 98.
69. Ibid., 99.
70. Ibid., 99 and 224n40. Knapp calls the ballet "the true linchpin of the film." Knapp, The American Musical, 77.
71. Ibid., 99.
72. Hanson, "Looking for Lela Simone," 833–34.
73. Ibid., 834.
74. Ibid., 831.
75. Alon, "It's Raining Films," unpaged.
76. Robert Cushman, "Singin' on the stage," Observer, July 3, 1983, 31.
77. See "London Musical Index," 1980–1984, accessed December 18, 2022, http://www.overthefootlights.co.uk/London_Musicals.html.
78. An earlier version of the show was a success in London's West End, opening in 1983. See also Benedict Nightingale, "Stage View; Yankee Products On The London Stage," New York Times, June 9, 1985, Section 2, Page 5. The first adaptation of an original film musical for Broadway was Gigi (1973). See Joshua Goodman, "Lerner and Loewe's Gigi: Context, Sources, and Performance"(PhD diss., University of Sheffield, 2022), chapter 4.
79. Jennifer Dunning, "Two Vintage Shows Are Reshaped For New Life On Broadway," New York Times, June 9, 1985, Section 2, Page 1.
80. Frank Rich, "The Stage: 'Singin' in The Rain' Opens," New York Times, July 3, 1985, C9.
81. Jack Barchas, "Singing Out," New York Times, July 28, 1985, Section 2, Page 12.
82. Samuel Freedman, "'Rain,' A Near-Failure, Has Vigorous Recovery," New York Times, September 9, 1985, C15.
83. Ibid.
84. Ibid.
85. Stanley Donen was the dance director on the film, produced by Joe Pasternak and directed by Laslo Benedik. The Kissing Bandit, AFI Catalog of Feature Films online.
86. See "London Musical Index," 2000–2004.
87. Ibid.; and Alex Wood, "Singin' in the Rain to embark on 2021 UK and Ireland Tour," WhatsOnStage, March 9, 2020, https://www.whatsonstage.com/cambridge-theatre/news/singin-in-the-rain-2021-uk-ireland-tour_51123.html.
88. Roslyn Sulcas, "Review: New 'Singin' in the Rain' in Paris Stays Faithful to the Original," New York Times, March 16, 2015, international edition.
89. Ibid.
90. Betty Comden quoted in Simi Horwitz, "Two 'On the Town,'" Backstage, November 11, 1998, 18.
91. Parts of this sequence were shot on location in New York City. A series of such visual references to lamp posts, Kelly's solo, and other classic film musicals pepper La La Land (2016)—see Hannah Lewis's study in this series.
92. Charles Champlin, "Kubrick's Vision of 'Clockwork,'" Los Angeles Times, December 21, 1971, E1.
93. The song was apparently originally suggested by McDowell, in consultation with Kubrick. Christine Lee Gengaro, Listening to Stanley Kubrick: The Music in His Films (Lanham, MD: Scarecrow Press, 2012), 41. My thanks to Geoffrey Block for this reference.

94. Nora Sayre, "'That's Entertainment' Certainly Is," *New York Times*, May 24, 1974, 22.

95. Robert Hilburn, "Music TV: Hope Rocks Fort Lee," *Los Angeles Times*, August 4, 1981, G1.

96. Patrick Goldstein, "The Pop Eye: James Accuses MTV Of Racism," *Los Angeles Times*, February 6, 1983), S88; and Wayne Robins, "Pop Music: A Thriller: Pop Battles Race Barrier," *Los Angeles Times*, August 7, 1983, R56.

97. Michael Goldberg, "Michael Jackson: The Making of 'the King of Pop,'" *Rolling Stone*, January 9, 1992, 32.

98. Michael Jackson, "Black or White," Official Video, accessed December 16, 2022, https://www.youtube.com/watch?v = pTFE8cirkdQ.

99. Coincidentally, Jackson maintained his own private zoo. Hannah Ellis-Petersen, "Michael Jackson Neverland Ranch expected to fetch up to $85m," *Guardian*, August 1, 2014, https://www.theguardian.com/music/2014/aug/01/michael-jackson-neverland-ranch-sell-50-million.

100. Ibid., 32.

101. Jon Pareles, "Review/Rock; New Video Opens the Jackson Blitz," *New York Times*, November 16, 1991, Section 1, Page 9. Pareles doesn't mention *Cover Girl* but does note that a character (played by actor/director Spike Lee) breaks a plate glass window with a garbage can at a crucial moment in a more proximate source, the film *Do the Right Thing* (1989).

102. Clover, "Dancin' in the Rain," 166.

103. Ibid., 157 and 162–65.

104. John O'Connor, "TV Reviews; 'American Film Institute Salute To Gene Kelly,'" *New York Times*, May 7, 1985, C22.

105. Hirschhorn, *Gene Kelly*, 138; cited in Dabholkar and Hess, *The Cinematic Voyage*, 143.

106. The Volkswagen Commercial "Singing in the Rain" with digitized dancers (2005), accessed December 18, 2022, https://www.youtube.com/watch?v = Myxb1f07cAo.

107. Kevin Roose, "It Was Only a Matter of Time: Here Comes an App for Fake Videos," *New York Times*, March 4, 2018, A1.

108. Mary Fogarty, "Gene Kelly: The Original, Updated," in *The Oxford Handbook of Dance and the Popular Screen*, ed. Melissa Blanco Borelli (New York: Oxford University Press, 2014), 91–92.

109. Ibid., 95.

110. Drawing upon previous articles by Franko (1989) and Bleeker (2012), Fogarty defines a "cover" as a "reconstruction" and a "remix" as a "reinvention." Ibid., 83–84 and 90.

111. Bernal also worked with Michael Jackson in 2009 in preparations for an upcoming concert tour. Jackson died before the tour could take place. See Charles Lam, "Elsewhere Man David Bernal, One of the Internet's First Dancing Stars," *OC Weekly*, March 20, 2015, accessed December 18, 2022, https://webcache.googleusercontent.com/search?q = cache:i2uSXzFZ2esJ:https://www.ocweekly.com/elsewhere-man-david-bernal-one-of-the-internets-first-dancing-stars-6569825/+&cd = 14&hl = en&ct = clnk&gl = uk. Regarding Counts's biography see Eric Vonheim, "Donnie 'Crumbs' Counts—Making of a B-Boy," Podcast, February 12, 2020, accessed December 18, 2022, https://www.youtube.com/watch?v = XdAFhpSFZIY. In another milestone in its globalization as a dance form, breaking was admitted as a competitive event at the 2024 Paris Olympiad.

112. See "George Sampson: Singing in The Rain —Britain's Got Talent 2008—The Final," accessed on December 18, 2022, https://www.youtube.com/watch?v = jq_ZIQ6vXps.

113. See Yuen on "colorblind racism, or the attribution of white dominance to individual merit and cultural explanations." Nancy Wang Yuen, *Reel Inequality: Hollywood Actors and Racism* (New Brunswick, NJ: Rutgers University Press, 2017), 50.

114. "Official Singles Chart Top 100 [June 8, 2008]," *The Official UK Chart Company*, accessed December 4, 2022, https://www.officialcharts.com/charts/singles-chart/20080608/7501/.

115. "New George Sampson Singing in The Rain Video" with George Sampson and a multiracial ensemble (posted 2009), accessed December 18, 2022, https://www.youtube.com/watch?v = CIrOiQr5EpA.

116. A later music video for the remix of "Singing in the Rain" by Mint Royale, unidentified dancer, also posted in 2009, accessed December 18, 2022, https://www.youtube.com/watch?v = IcYa9b7mMmA.

117. George Sampson on *Britain's Got Talent: The Champions* (21/9/19), accessed December 18, 2022, https://www.youtube.com/watch?v = D1p2hZE4EEA.

118. "Audition," Fox Network, *Glee*, season 2, episode 1, aired September 21, 2010, https://www.imdb.com/title/tt1628297/.

119. "The Substitute," Fox Network, *Glee,* season 2, episode 7, aired November 16, 2010, https://web.archive.org/web/20101210094604/http://www.fox.com/glee/recaps/season-2/episode-7.

120. "Umbrella (Orange Version) (Official Music Video)," YouTube, December 14, 2009; Music video for "Umbrella" (2007, by Christopher Stewart et al.), performed by Rihanna and Jay-Z; accessed December 5, 2022, https://www.youtube.com/watch?v = CvBfHwUxHIk

121. Chris Burden, *Urban Light* (2008), outdoor sculpture, Los Angeles County Museum of Art, https://collections.lacma.org/node/214966.

122. Pdogg [Kang Hyo-won] et al., "Boy With Luv," performed by BTS, music video directed by YongSeok Choi (Big Hit Entertainment, 2019), https://www.youtube.com/watch?v = XsX3ATc3FbA.

123. MegaForce [advertising agency], "Pushing Boundaries," commercial for Burberry, November 20, 2020, accessed April 26, 2023, https://www.youtube.com/watch?v = QdC8jx1jr5A&ab_channel = KBNNextMedia. See also Sophie Walker, "On the Rise: Dreya Mac," *Best Fit,* April 15, 2021, accessed December 18, 2022, https://www.thelineofbestfit.com/features/interviews/dreya-mac-on-the-rise. My thanks to *Gigi* scholar Joshua Goodman for alerting me to this novel remix.

124. Sara Spary, "Burberry Reimagines 'Singin' in the Rain' in Glorious Celebration of London's Gray, Gritty Streets," *AdWeek,* November 12, 2020, accessed December 22, 2022, https://www.adweek.com/creativity/burberry-reimagines-singin-in-the-rain-in-glorious-celebration-of-londons-gray-gritty-streets/; "(La)Horde" biographies, accessed December 22, 2022, https://www.ballet-de-marseille.com/en/biography; and "What We Do," Lank & Tank, accessed December 22, 2022, https://www.lankandtank.com/what-we-do.

125. Manohla Dargis, "Excess Hollywood: All Partying, Little Life," *New York Times,* December. 23, 2022, C 6C6; and Devon Coggan, "Every *Singin' in the Rain* Reference in *Babylon,*" *(Entertainment Weekly,* December 26, 2022), https://ew.com/movies/babylon-singin-in-the-rain-references/. Regarding Diggs in *Extrapolations* see James Poniewozik, "Urgency Can't Be Optional," *New York Times,* April 1, 2023, C1; and "Extrapolations Season 1, Episode 3 2047: The Fifth Question Transcript," accessed April 23, 2023, at: https://tvshowtranscripts.ourboard.org/viewtopic.php?t=61466t=61466.

126. Chris Garcia, "Cyd Charisse's glorious feeling; 'Singin' in the Rain' co-star recalls her last-minute chance to dance with Gene Kelly," *Austin American Statesman,* September 27, 2002, E3.

127. Vincent Canby, "Film View: A Joyously Indestructible Movie Returns," *New York Times,* May 4, 1975, D15.

128. Lewis, *"Love Me Tonight (1932),"* 5. See also Geoffrey Block's guide to the film, and Lewis's volume on *La La Land,* other titles in this series, and Geoffrey Block, "Integration."

129. Lewis, 4, on aesthetic unity, and Richard Rodgers regarding orchestration and costumes in *Oklahoma!,* quoted in Lewis, 5; see also Richard Rodgers, *Musical Stages* (New York: Random House, 1975), 227.

130. Lewis, 4.

131. In addition to the examples discussed in this chapter see the documentary "Raining on a New Generation" (2012) included on the 2-DVD release of *Singin'.*

132. "Theater Talk: Remembering Betty Comden."

Bibliography

Archival Abbreviations

AL = Margaret Herrick Library, Academy of Motion Pictures Arts and Sciences, Los Angeles
BU = Howard Gottlieb Archives, Boston University
NYPL = New York Public Library, Performing Arts Research Collections at Lincoln Center; primarily the Billy Rose Theatre Collection
USC = Cinematic Library, University of Southern California, Los Angeles

Books and Articles

Alon, Talya. "It's Raining Films: Intertextuality in Singin' in the Rain." *Literature/Film Quarterly* 45, no. 3 (2021): unpaged; accessed April 22, 2023, https://lfq.salisbury.edu/_iss ues/45_3/its_raining_films.html.

Altman, Rick, ed. *Genre, the Musical.* London: Routledge & Kegan Paul, 1981.

Baer, William. *Classic American Films: Conversations with the Screenwriters.* Westport, CT: Praeger, 2008, 1–17. This interview was first published in *Michigan Quarterly Review* 41, no. 1 (2002): 1–20; accessed September 3, 2019, http://hdl.handle.net/2027/spo.act2 080.0041.101.

Basinger, Jeanine. *The Movie Musical!* New York: Knopf, 2019.

Behlmer, Rudy. *America's Favorite Movies, Behind the Scenes.* New York: Frederick Ungar, 1982.

Bingen, Steven, et al. *MGM: Hollywood's Greatest Backlot.* Solana Beach, CA: Santa Monica Press, 2011.

Blair, Betsy. *The Memory of All That: Love and Politics in New York, Hollywood, and Paris.* New York: Alfred A. Knopf, 2003.

Block, Geoffrey, "Integration," in *The Oxford Handbook of the American Musical,* ed. by Raymond Knapp, Mitchell Morris, and Stacy Wolf, 97–110. New York: Oxford University Press, 2011.

Broomfield-McHugh, Dominic, ed. *The Oxford Handbook of the Hollywood Musical.* New York: Oxford University Press, 2022.

Casper, Joseph Andrew. *Stanley Donen.* Metuchen, NJ: Scarecrow Press, 1983.

Chabrol, Claude. "Que Ma Joie Demeure [That My Joy Remains]." *Cahiers du Cinéma* 5, no. 28 (November 1953): 55–57.

Charisse, Cyd, and Tony Martin. *The Two of Us.* New York: Mason/Charter, 1976.

Charness, Casey. "Hollywood Cine-Dance: A Description of the Interrelationship of Camerawork and Choreography in Films by Stanley Donen and Gene Kelly." PhD diss., New York University, 1977.

Chin, Elizabeth. "Michael Jackson's Panther Dance: Double Consciousness and the Uncanny Business of Performing While Black." *Journal of Popular Music Studies* 23, no. 1 (March 2011): 58–74.

Clover, Carol. "Dancin' in the Rain." *Critical Inquiry* 21, no. 4 (Summer 1995): 722–47; reprinted in *Hollywood Musicals, The Film Reader,* edited by Steven Cohan, 157–73. New York: Routledge, 2001.

Comden, Betty, and Adolph Green. *Singin' in the Rain: Story and Screenplay.* Introduction by the authors. New York: Viking Press, 1972.

Dabholkar, Pratibha A., and Earl J. Hess. *"Singin' in the Rain": The Making of an American Masterpiece.* Lawrence: University of Kansas Press, 2009.

Dabholkar, Pratibha A., and Earl J. Hess. *The Cinematic Voyage of* The Pirate: *Kelly, Garland, and Minnelli at Work.* Columbia: University of Missouri Press, 2014.

Dabholkar, Pratibha A., and Earl J. Hess. *Gene Kelly: The Making of a Creative Legend.* Lawrence: University Press of Kansas, 2020.

Dabholkar, Pratibha A., and Earl J. Hess. *Gene Kelly's Invitation to the Dance: The Auteur and the Dance Film in Hollywood's Golden Age.* Available on Academia.edu, 2023.

Daniell, Tina, and Pat McGilligan. "Betty Comden and Adolph Green: Almost Improvisation." In *Backstory 2: Interviews with Screenwriters of the 1940s and 1950s,* edited by Pat McGilligan, 73–88. Berkeley: University of California Press, 1991.

de Lucas, Cristina. "Dancing Happiness: Lyrics and Choreography in Singin' in the Rain (1952)." In "Writing Dancing/Dancing Writing." *SDHS Proceedings,* Thirty-seventh Annual International Conference, Iowa City, IA, November 13–16, 2014, 59–66.

Decker, Todd. *Music Makes Me: Fred Astaire and Jazz.* Berkeley: University of California Press, 2011.

Delamater, Jerome. *Dance in the Hollywood Musical.* Ann Arbor, MI: UMI Research Press, 1981.

Denfeld, Duane Colt. "Future Hollywood Producer Arthur Freed Performs at Camp Lewis Jewish Welfare House on May 21, 1918." *History Link,* Essay 11087 (August 19, 2015), https://dev.historylink.org/File/11087.

Doherty, Thomas. *Hollywood's Censor: Joseph I. Breen and the Production Code Administration.* New York: Columbia University Press, 2007.

Eyman, Scott. *The Lion of Hollywood.* New York: Simon & Schuster, 2005.

Feuer, Jane. *The Hollywood Musical.* 2nd Ed. Bloomington: Indiana University Press, 1993.

Feuer, Jane. "The Self-Reflexive Musical and the Myth of Entertainment." In *Film Genre Reader II,* edited by Barry Keith Grant, 444–51. Austin: University of Texas Press,1995.

Fordin, Hugh. *MGM's Greatest Musicals: The Arthur Freed Unit.* New York: Da Capo Press, 1996 (1975).

Genné, Beth. "The Film Musicals of Vincente Minnelli and the Team of Gene Kelly and Stanley Donen: 1944–1958." Ph.D. diss., University of Michigan, 1984.

Genné, Beth. *Dance Me a Song: Astaire, Balanchine, Kelly, and the American Film Musical.* New York: Oxford University Press, 2018.

Gottschild, Brenda Dixon. *Digging the Africanist Presence in American Performance: Dance and Other Contexts.* Westport, CT: Greenwood Press, 1996.

Grosch, Nils. "Musical Comedy, Pastiche and the Challenge of 'Rewriting.'" In *Intertextuality in Music: Dialogic Composition,* edited by Violetta Kostka, Paulo de Castro, and William Everett, 156–66. New York: Routledge, 2021.

Grosch, Nils, and Joachim Brügge, editors. *"Singin' in the Rain": Kulturgeschichte eines Hollywood-Musical-Klassikers [Cultural History of a Hollywood Musical Classic].* Münster and New York: Waxmann, 2014.

Hanson, Helen. "Looking for Lela Simone: *Singin' in the Rain* and Microhistories of Women's Sound Work behind the Scenes and Below-the-line in Classical Hollywood Cinema." *Women's History Review* 29, no. 5 (2020): 822–40.

Hirschhorn, Clive. *Gene Kelly: A Biography.* New York: St. Martin's Press, 1984 (1974).

Ireland, David. "Singin' Over Rainbows: The Incongruent Film Song and Extra-filmic Reception." *The Soundtrack* 7, no. 2 (2014): 119–32.

Johnson, Albert. "Conversation with Roger Edens. *Sight and Sound* 27, no. 4 (Spring 1958): 179–82.

Kelly, Gillian. "Gene Kelly: The Performing Auteur—Manifestations of the Kelly Persona." *eSharp* (2010): 136–56.

Knapp, Raymond. *The American Musical and the Performance of Personal Identity.* Princeton, NJ: Princeton University Press, 2009.

Knight, Arthur. *Disintegrating the Musical: Black Performance and American Musical Film.* Durham, NC: Duke University Press, 2002.

Knox, Donald. *The Magic Factory: How MGM Made "An American in Paris."* Foreword by Andrew Sarris. New York: Praeger, 1973.

Kraut, Anthea Kraut. *Choreographing Copyright: Race, Gender, and Intellectual Property Rights in American Dance.* New York: Oxford University Press, 2016.

Lewis, Hannah. "*Love Me Tonight (1932)* and the Development of the Integrated Film Musical." *Musical Quarterly* 100, no. 1 (Spring 2017): 3–32.

Mordden, Ethan. *The Hollywood Musical.* New York: St. Martin's Press, 1981.

Nadel, Alan. *Demographic Angst: Cultural Narrative and American Films of the 1950s.* New Brunswick, NJ: Rutgers University Press, 2018.

Reynolds, Debbie, and David Patrick Columbia. *Debbie: My Life.* New York: William Morrow, 1988.

Schatz, Thomas. *The Genius of the System: Hollywood Filmmaking in the Studio Era.* Foreword by Steven Bach. Minneapolis: University of Minnesota Press, 2010 (1988).

Silverman, Stanley. *Dancing on the Ceiling: Stanley Donen and His Movies.* With an introduction by Audrey Hepburn. New York: Alfred A. Knopf, 1996.

Travis, Doris Eaton, with Joseph and Charles Eaton, as told to J. R. Morris. *The Days We Danced: The Story of My Theatrical Family from Florenz Ziegfeld to Arthur Murray and Beyond.* Seattle: Marquand Books, 2003.

Westover, Jonas. "'Be a Clown' and 'Make 'Em Laugh': Comic Timing, Rhythm, and Donald O'Connor's Face." In *Sounding Funny: Sound and Comedy Cinema,* edited by Mark Evans and Philip Heyward, 122–47. Sheffield, UK, and Bristol, CT: Equinox Publishing, 2016.

Whitesell, Lloyd. *Wonderful Design: Glamour in the Hollywood Musical.* New York: Oxford University Press, 2018.

Wollen, Peter. *Singin' in the Rain.* Reissued with a New Foreword by Geoff Andrew. London: Palgrave Macmillan, 2012 (1992).

Filmography and Discography

"An Evening with Gene Kelly." Interview with Gavin Millar. BBC, 1974, accessed December 12, 2022, https://www.youtube.com/watch?v=M31tPymsGpw.

Singin' in the Rain, the documentaries: *"What a Glorious Feeling: The Making of Singin' in the Rain," "Musicals Great Musicals—The Arthur Freed Unit at MGM," "Singin' in the Rain—Raining on a New Generation,"* a fifty-minute-long reel of songs from the film as performed in earlier films, and photos and extant video and audio recordings of cut musical numbers. Burbank, CA: Warner Home Video/Turner Entertainment Co., 2002 (1952), 2-DVD set.

Singin' in the Rain, original motion picture soundtrack, with extant audio outtakes and alternate takes. Turner Entertainment Company, 2002, 2-CD set.

"*Singin' in the Rain* 50th Anniversary." Panel Discussion. AMPAS, 2002, accessed November 23, 2022, https://www.oscars.org/search/site/Panel%20Discussion%2C%20%22Singin%27%20in%20the%20Rain%2050th%20Anniversary.

"Theater Talk: Remembering Betty Comden." With Michael Riedel and Susan Haskins. Theater Talk Productions and CUNY-TV, December 1, 2006, accessed December 8, 2022, https://www.youtube.com/watch?v=8TTyCBacP8U.

Other Resources

AFI Catalog of Feature Films, https://aficatalog.afi.com/.

Internet Broadway Database, https://www.ibdb.com/.

US Bureau of Labor Statistics, "CPI Inflation Calculator," https://www.bls.gov/data/inflation_calculator.htm.

Index